A COUPLE'S JOURNEY TO TRANSGENDERISM

NOREEN ANTAO

A COUPLE'S JOURNEY TO TRANSGENDERISM

NOREEN ANTAO

TABLE OF CONTENTS

ACKNOWLEDGEMENTS

For Book Design, Cover Design, and Editing — Stu Segal

A special thank you to:

My heterosexual {male} crossdresser friends for candidly sharing their experiences of living in our often homophobic society.

All the wives and significant others of crossdressers I have met over the last six years. Your love, support, and sharing of your life experiences makes me humble.

My two sons; you have grown to be loving, kind, and accepting young adults. I am blessed and proud to have you in my life. Thanks for being so patient with me during the writing of this book.

Claudia Baez, my favorite Bartender at the Bar of Bishop, for your love, support and friendship.

Evvy Frazier, you are the sister I only hoped to have; and being my sister-in-Christ too, makes me doubly blessed. I feel privileged to be the one chosen to guide you in your walk with Christ. You have always been there for me. Words cannot express my gratitude to you.

Thanks for keeping me laughing, Blanca, Marco, and the rest of the Garcia sisters; Rosa, Linda, and Iris. I thank you for including me in your family. I love you all.

Robert "Stonewall" Jackson, I appreciate the honor of writing your book, "The Life and Legend of Robert 'Stonewall' Jackson." You are truly an amazing young man at the age of 71. I appreciate you being my personal body trainer and a very good friend. Thanks for sharing your grandchildren with me; I have enjoyed spending time with you and Prince, Nasjah, and Nigel, whom I love dearly.

Gus Wright, you are a true man of God. I appreciate your wisdom, rational thinking, and tackling of difficult issues. I have tremendous respect for you.

INTRODUCTION

Alcoholism ran in my family, and although I never intended to repeat this cycle, my first marriage was to an alcoholic. I suffered physical and mental abuse at his hands. I have two beautiful sons through this marriage. I divorced him after ten years of marriage wanting to make sure my sons would not end up influenced by their father's disease. My second chance at love came when I met a man I knew I wanted to marry. He was a gentle and sensitive person, who I felt would make a loving husband and a great dad to my two young sons. One day my starry-eyed world turned upside down when my prince charming told me about a skeleton hidden, buried deep down, in his closet for thirty-three years. What he told me changed all our lives.

This book follows the ups and downs of being married to a heterosexual crossdresser. It is my desire to tell my story in the hope it helps other genetic women who discover that the man they love is a crossdresser. Also, my experiences will help other women faced with the decision of whether to stay in the relationship or to distance themselves as quickly as possible.

For many genetic women, the decision to stay or leave is primarily based on the pressure of living a life considered taboo by our society.

I hope this book is used to aid other heterosexual crossdressers married or in relationships with genetic women. It will give them a better understanding of what their wives and significant others go through when they choose to remain in such relationships.

Many of our young teenage boys and girls grow up knowing they are different. The initial thought is that they are gay. They openly come out and live the gay life. After a while, they realize they are still missing something. Many of them take their own lives. I hope this book helps them or their parents to open up to the possibility that they may be a crossdresser.

Some of my dear friends are heterosexual male crossdressers. I have attended various events with them over the years. In Dallas, there is a heterosexual male group that requires its members to be heterosexual married males. The male applicant has to go through an interview and screening process.

The group welcomes and encourages their wives and significant others to participate in group events, however, very few attend. I had discussions with several of the wives and significant others as to why they didn't participate. Responses varied, the most common being "I am uncomfortable being seen with my crossdresser" or "I am afraid my neighbors and friends will recognize me." The genetic ladies who do attend these events are usually disguised. It was not uncommon to see some wearing wigs and sunglasses.

I began a quest to discover why heterosexual male crossdressers feel different from other males. Why is it that they find more pleasure and satisfaction from dressing as females? Is it for sexual pleasure? Could it be their insecurities, disgust looking at their male organs; or are their brains wired differently from other males?

Crossdressers coming out for the very first time are filled with joy and excitement. The joy and excitement they feel dressed as a female makes them extremely emotional. Since childhood, they dreamed of this day and now it has become a reality. The similarity in their stories is uncanny. Most discover at a very young age that they are different from other males. The most common response I have received is, "We are female trapped in a male's body."

Our society welcomes the strides women have taken. Traditionally, women are given more leeway in their choice of clothing, jobs, and hairstyles. For heterosexual males, this is not the case. We live in a society that deems it unacceptable for a male to express his feminine side by dressing as a female, yet accepts a woman dressed in male clothing.

Most people who negatively judge crossdressers base their prejudice on their religious beliefs. Crossdressers do not fit society's opinion of what constitutes 'normal.' I too struggled with my religious beliefs on this subject. However, over the years, I have developed tremendous compassion for people in pain. Especially those who struggle with emotional issues. For me, it is important to consider their loving hearts and concern for each other.

Listed below are the commonly accepted definitions of words related to "heterosexual," which can be confusing to some of us:

HETERO-SEXUAL: Exclusively attracted to the opposite sex. (Boys/men like girls/women—and vice versa).

BI-SEXUAL: Man or woman attracted to both sexes.

HOMO-SEXUAL: Exclusively attracted to the same sex. (Men like men) (Women like women). The word "Homosexual" can be offensive to many.

GAY: Men or women attracted to the same sex. "Lesbian" is the preferred term for women attracted to women.

TRANSSEXUAL: A person who has undergone hormone treatment and surgery to attain the physical characteristics of the opposite sex.

TRANSGENDER: Denoting or relating to a person whose self-identity does not conform unambiguously to conventional notions of male or female gender.

Can There Really Be Life After Divorce?

Wednesday evenings are always the highlight of my week. I get to meet my dear friends Evvy, Blanca, and bartender Claudia for happy hour at our favorite place, the Bar of Bishop in the Bishop Arts District in Dallas, Texas. My favorite frozen alcoholic beverage called a Mango Sumui is half-priced all evening long.

Evvy is a new believer in Christ. Our discussions usually revolve around how she is growing in her walk with Christ. Like all new believers, Evvy faces many challenges dealing with friends and acquaintances who are non-believers. I enjoy talking to Evvy, as she reminds me of myself when I first became a believer. I remember having to take baby steps to learn more about the bible. I gained knowledge by spending time in bible studies and fellowship with mature women believers in the church.

Today was a hot Wednesday afternoon in Dallas. The temperatures were already scorching with no breeze in the air for relief. It was a perfect hot afternoon for a Mango Sumui. Since I had a few hours to kill before Evvy got there, I debated on whether to go home to take a nap or head straight to the bar to visit with my favorite bartender, Claudia. The Bar won because it was closer. I decided to walk instead of driving. I am a petite lady, probably no more than five feet tall, with short dark brown hair. I was wearing white jeans with a hot pink shirt, opened low enough to show cleavage. I could feel the shirt hugging my body drenched in perspiration. My hair was soaking wet and perspiration was dripping down my face, ruining any trace of makeup that was left. As I got to the bar's parking lot, I realized walking was a mistake. I remember thinking, "How foolish of me to walk on a hot dry Dallas summer afternoon. I'll never do this again."

As I entered the bar it took my eyes a few minutes to adjust to the dim lights that gave the place an illusion of romance. As my eyes adjusted to the dimly lit room, I rushed into the restroom to freshen up. I felt grateful for leaving an antiperspirant at the bar, it sure came in handy today. I came out of the restroom and perched myself on a bar stool in my regular spot. I wanted to relax and enjoy the cool air blowing through the vent from the ceiling above and sip an ice-cold Mango Sumui. I looked around for Claudia but she was nowhere in sight.

Claudia finally emerged and was surprised to see me this early in the afternoon. She poured me my favorite frozen mango drink and we spent time talking to each other. Then she motioned me toward a lady sitting at the far end of the bar. Claudia whispered, "She is a new customer, go introduce yourself to her as she seems to be alone?"

With a smile, I said, "Claudia, what am I, your bar greeter now? Besides, you are the bartender you should be talking to her." "You are the bubbly, outgoing one with a knack for putting people at ease," Claudia responded, walking off.

I am a regular at the bar that I refer to as 'my neighborhood bar.' Over time, I became comfortable enough that I began to introduce myself to new customers, welcome them in, and engage them in conversation to make their first visit enjoyable. This started a trend. Other regulars, who were once new, began welcoming newcomers to the bar.

I walked over and as I got closer, I saw she was quite attractive. She flashed me a big warm smile. I held out my hand and introduced myself to her and she did the same. Since I had plenty of time to spare, I sat by her and we talked for at least an hour. I glanced at my watch and saw it was 5:30. Evvy should be leaving work in 15 minutes. Right enough, fifteen minutes later Evvy arrived. Introductions were made and the three of us were soon chatting like old friends.

It was now 8:00 pm and the bar didn't close until 10:00 pm. I was getting extremely tired and thankfully we all decided to call it a night. We paid our tabs and waved goodbye to Claudia, who was busy behind the bar.

I started to walk towards home, when Evvy grabbed my arm, saying, "No way are you walking in this heat again. Let me drive you home."

I was too tired to argue with Evvy; I got into her car. "Now wasn't that a lovely evening?" said Evvy. "It sure was," I agreed with my eyes closed.

Most of my friends tell me I have an outgoing, bubbly personality. When I walk into a room, it's like a burst of sunshine. Over the years, as my life changed drastically, I learned to use humor to disguise my pain. I was successful for the most part, as most of my friends and family hadn't noticed that the bubbliness had become a facade.

Since my divorce from an alcoholic husband, I lost the desire to meet single men. My friends of course tried to change things for me.

One Sunday after mass, my friend Debra said to me. "Why don't you join our church singles group? You will meet other divorced women learning to be single again".

"Debra," I said, shocked, "you know I can't do that. I am not ready to be around men just yet." "Then stay away from the men," countered Debra. "Make friends with the women in the group".

Debra headed to the stack of church bulletins lying on a table nearby, picked one up, and handed it to me.

"Details in there," she said. "Now make sure you at least try it out. You don't have to go again if you don't like it."

When I returned home from church, I made myself a cup of coffee and flopped in my favorite chair with the bulletin in hand. I glanced through the singles section and found an event that seemed interesting. A group was meeting at the church and had a car-pooling arrangement. I disliked driving long distances at night so this seemed just right for me.

I called the number listed in the bulletin. A man answered. I was shaking with nervousness and could barely speak.

"I am recently divorced," I managed to say. "I would like to know more about the event this coming weekend."

He introduced himself to me as John. "I know you are very nervous and hesitant. We all were when we first joined the group." His voice was gentle and put me at ease. "There are several members in our group who have gone through a divorce including myself. I understand what you are going through. The members of the group will as well. We have survived with support from others. The friendships and love we developed in this group was the therapy we all needed". Now almost in tears I said, "John, I will be at the event this weekend." "Great," John said. "We would love to have you visit us." When I put the phone down I was still shaking.

I came from a large supportive family and had a decent job. What I needed most was to make new single friends. Most of the church events were held on weekends. I could only attend those when my sons were with their father. I longed to have friends with whom I could take in a movie or dinner on the weekends when the boys were gone. Most of my friends are married and busy with their own lives. However, some still made time to have dinner with me occasionally. Unfortunately, their conversations usually revolved around their marriages and date nights with their husbands. They also talked about fun monthly dinners with friends that included their husbands. They insisted I join them, but I felt like a fish out of water at these dinners. My life had changed significantly. These conversations made me depressed. It felt like they were insensitive to my situation of being single again.

On the night of the church singles event, I suffered an anxiety attack. The single life was so new to me. It made me vacillate between "Should I go or should I stay home?" I paced back and forth in my living room. Eventually, with determination I lifted up my fears in prayer, asking for the courage to move on with my life. I felt calmer and my anxiety lessened. I left home and headed to the church.

When I entered the meeting room, I counted at least ten people already there. This surprised me. I expected at the most, only five or six would show up. I was introduced to the group members who were very friendly. They seemed to understand what I was going through. Their comments were really heartening.

"You will survive the divorce, we all did." "We will help you put this divorce behind you. We will be with you through the healing process and you will find happiness again."

"You know there is life after divorce. You will come to this place when you are ready."

As the event came to an end, I had a list of names and telephone numbers. Men and women told me to call them anytime I needed something or someone or just to talk. I was amazed at how comfortable they made me feel.

Some of the men who knew I had two young sons offered to include them in the group events.

"We are planning a group event this month to attend a Ranger's baseball game. We would be happy to have your boys sit by us during the game and to answer any questions that come up."

Since there were several women signed up to go, I signed up too. I felt my boys would feel more comfortable if I was with them. "Thanks so much. I plan to take you up on the offer."

The event was in the planning stages. This would give me enough time to get the boys warmed up to the idea.

Every weekend that I didn't have my boys, I attended group events. After socializing with the group members at various events, I decided to become an active member and get more involved.

I heard through the grapevine that one of the previous presidents had resigned because he was to marry a member of the group. Four months after I joined, the current president also resigned for the same reason. She too fell in love with a group member. Their plans were to get married shortly.

The current president and a couple of group members approached me to discuss the election of a new president. The other members felt confident I would make a great president. "Noreen, you have great social skills and you are very popular with the members."

I was stunned. I hadn't been with the group long. What were they thinking? "We feel you would make a great president," said Ricky one of the members who came along with the president to see me. "We need someone like you to step up and take charge of our group. You have an outgoing personality. You will be successful in increasing the membership of our group. Also, we need to increase the participation at our group events. You are so much fun to be around and everybody in the group already loves you." I was apprehensive, but in the end decided to run for president. I had only one opponent in the election. Once all the votes were cast, I was named the winner. I was voted in as the new president. There were quite a few jokes of, "You are not going to fall in love with a group member right? We lost our previous two presidents who married group members."

I laughed in reply. "It has taken me ten years to finally get my freedom back. Now why would you even think I'd give it up to get married again? I am finally enjoying being single, and the freedom that comes with it."

I went back to being myself, outgoing, friendly, and genuinely concerned for those in pain. Making friends came natural to me. I always have had a heart for the shy ones. I have spent a considerable amount of time helping them overcome their shyness. I understand how difficult it is for them to make friends. At all events, I make sure to sit by the shy visitors. I gradually introduced them to a few members at a time. I was confident these group members would make the visitors feel comfortable. Most of the members themselves were very shy when they first joined the group. I felt introducing the visitors to the whole group at one time could be intimidating, not to mention overwhelming.

After each event, I stayed back to speak to the new visitors. "Did you have a good time tonight? Were you comfortable talking to the people sitting by you? The friends you made tonight including me would love to see you return. Call me anytime you feel shy or uncomfortable attending an event alone."

I returned phone calls from singles who had called and left messages while my kids were in bed asleep. Most of the messages were from singles needing information on the group. It was not unusual for me to spend 45 minutes on the phone convincing a single to attend an event.

One week before Halloween I decided to host a pizza dinner for the group. The place I selected was a restaurant, further away from the usual spots near the church. It was not uncommon for a member to host a dinner event closer to their home. The decision on a place to eat was typically based on how familiar the members were with the menu and the staff.

I picked this restaurant for its architectural design resembling a quaint cottage. The inside of the place was uniquely designed. The dining area was broken into several rooms separated by beautiful arched walls. These rooms provided a private atmosphere. The restaurant was famous for deep dish pizzas, however, they also offered a small selection of thin crust which is my favorite.

One member, Julie, complained about my decision. "The traffic is too heavy around dinner time, driving there stresses me out." Ricky, another member, chimed in "Why don't we carpool to the restaurant? I feel we need to venture out and try something different rather than, eating at the same old places." The rest of the group agreed the pizza place was a great idea. Like Julie, I too didn't like driving in heavy traffic.

On the day of the event, everyone met in the church parking lot and piled into Ricky's van. Several of the group members decided they would drive their own cars and meet up at the pizza place. As Ricky drove into the parking lot of the restaurant Julie was excited.

"This place looks like a cottage from one of the fairytale books I read as a child." I was glad Julie was happy with the place. Most of the time, Julie was negative and found something to complain about. The evening began with a magician dressed in a black long-tailed tuxedo, white gloves and a tall black hat. He came to our table and started performing magic tricks for us. The magician continued with several more tricks, probably because the group members were generously tipping him.

I was pleased to see them having a good time. While the magic show was still in progress, I noticed a man walking into the pizza place. He was heading straight towards our table. When he got to the table, he greeted one of the group members, Joe. Judging from the interaction between the two, it was obvious they had previously met.

Joe walked over to where I was sitting and introduced his friend Jason to me. Jason was a clean-cut, all-American Caucasian standing at 5'8". He was wearing a light blue long-sleeved cotton shirt. His casual pants, once navy blue, were now faded blue and two sizes larger. The shoes hugging his feet appeared to be heavily worn and faded. I could tell his pants and shoes had seen better days. His hair color was dark brown, cut short, and styled like a young boy. I thought to myself, "This guy could use a haircut styled to flatter his face." The eyeglasses he was wearing appeared to be heavy. A steel frame encircled thick lenses. The eyeglasses were way too big for his face.

A quick observation of his mannerisms told me he was painfully shy. Jason made very little eye contact with me when I spoke to him. He seemed to be very awkward as he was playing with his keys. His keys were on a key ring attached to a long heavy silver chain. The chain was fastened to one of his belt loops on the left. The keys on this chain-hung way below his knee and jangled when he walked. He had a fixed smile and if one didn't know better, they would have sworn it was tattooed on his face.

He had scars on his face which were probably the result of having acne as a teenager. The scars were very similar to the ones on my friend's face. My friend had acne when he was a teenager which was the result of picking at his face. Jason's body frame was small and skinny. His physical appearance could improve if he gained more weight.

Jason recently moved to Dallas from Washington on a job offer. He had been living in Dallas for approximately three months. He visited the group to make new friends.

I felt drawn to Jason. There was something about him that intrigued me. I could not put my finger on it just yet. I hoped by attending the group events regularly, it would force him to interact with other members and get over his shyness sooner. Jason was introduced to the people sitting by him and he seemed to be at ease joining in on the conversation.

When I had the chance to speak to Jason again, I said "I volunteered to help for upcoming events announced at our monthly meetings. This helped me make friends quicker and my friendships have grown stronger ever since then."

In the group, there were several women who were very visual when it came to men. They only dated the good-looking guys. These women were shallow and wouldn't give Jason the time of day. Unlike me, they didn't invest time searching beneath the surface for the man's heart and soul.

A New Friend

That night I invited Jason and a few others to a Halloween dance held at one of the local Catholic churches. Jason declined the invitation and said, "I do not wear costumes and I don't know how to dance."

On the night of the event, I was surprised to see him. He was wearing the same clothes he wore at last week's dinner. I walked up to him smiling.

"Where is your costume?" "I'm wearing it," he smiled. I laughed at his dry sense of humor.

The dance was being held at a school gymnasium associated with the church. The place began filling up with singles from other surrounding churches. There were many people at the party wearing costumes which was exciting to watch. Many of the singles put on their thinking caps and created some of the most amazing costumes.

The other girls and I tried to get Jason on the dance floor. "Jason it's so simple, we can teach you how to dance." "I have told you all I do not have any rhythm nor do I have dancing feet," he insisted.

And he was right. This became fairly obvious once he hit the dance floor. He just stood there trying his best to move. This only made him look more pathetic.

I refused to give up on him. "Jason I am about to stick my fingers in the belt loops of your pants. We will be facing each other. I am determined to teach you how to dance."

I stuck my fingers in the belt loops of his pants and we stood facing each other. I began swaying to the music, and Jason hung on for dear life. He was a good sport and finally made some progress. He enjoyed the attention he was getting from the girls. His confidence level was rising and he attempted to do the Macarena. To my surprise, he did extremely well. After this, he was fairly relaxed and enjoyed the rest of the evening.

Later that night the winner of the costume contest would be announced. They were judging based on the most creative costume. I dressed as Betty from the Flintstones. I was very proud of the costume I made for this event. My jewelry was made from the bones of the chicken we ate the night before.

The costume contest came to an end and the judges picked a winner. The winner was Nathan, a member of our group. His costume was a very tight red one-piece suit worn by professional bicycles. He walked around with his helmet in one hand. The crowd booed at the judges, they felt Nathan's costume was not creative. The judges refused to change their decision. Nathan won two dinner tickets to The Mansion in Dallas.

As Jason and I spent more time together, our friendship grew stronger. We became comfortable sharing bits and pieces of our personal lives with each other.

One night after a group potluck dinner Jason cleaned up the kitchen. It was now 1:00 am. Jason didn't show any signs of leaving.

"Jason, I am extremely tired. I would like nothing better than to change into my PJs and get some sleep. There is a spare bedroom you can use if you plan to spend the night."

When I returned wearing my PJs I saw all the lights in the house still on. It was not like Jason to leave without turning all the lights off. I walked through the house turning off lights. When I reached the living room, he was still sitting in the spot where I'd left him earlier. He was deep in thought.

I walked into the kitchen and made myself a pot of hot tea. I returned with a steaming cup of tea in hand. I sat down Indian-style on my couch across from him. Finally, I asked. "What's on your mind? You obviously have something to say to me?" He stared at me for quite a while. He was not sure if he could trust me with what he was about to say. "I joined the singles group for several reasons he said. The main reason was to meet a girl, fall in love, and eventually get married. I'd like to meet a woman about my height with blonde hair." In retrospect, I realized he was trying to tell me about his alternate life. He seemed to have changed his mind. Maybe he was afraid he'd lose me as a friend.

I was disappointed hearing this, however, I decided to be completely honest. "If you want to marry a blonde bombshell, you need to change the way you look and dress."

He was listening, so I went on. "Your complexion is very pale. Most of the shirts you wear are pastel colors. This combination pretty much makes you look washed out. You blend in with the colors of your shirts. You need to get some serious help shopping for clothes. Your clothes need to suit your complexion and your size which will make you stand out more. Wearing your pants two sizes larger, your keys attached to a chain hanging down from your pant loop and, those worn-out shoes, all that needs to go."

He laughed, "I can always find my keys when I need them, can you say that about yourself?" I looked at him and rolled my eyes. He laughed again.

"Okay, okay, thank you for your advice. I appreciate it. So when can we go shopping? I obviously have no sense of fashion but you seem to do?"

I found myself laughing too and said, "Of course, I will go shopping with you. Would this weekend work for you?"

I knew he was very tight with his money. I smiled at him and said, "It'll be fun going shopping with you. I will enjoy seeing you spend your money."

We spent the next several weekends shopping for him. He purchased clothes, socks, and shoes. Finding shoes for Jason that fit his feet comfortably was extremely frustrating. He was very selective and picky with the type of shoes he wore. It took us hours of visiting several different shoe stores only to walk away with no purchase. Finally, he found the shoes he liked that were comfortable. He headed toward the counter with two shoe boxes in hand. "Yea! Mission accomplished Amen," I yelled.

He looked at me and burst into laughter. The other customers who were around joined in on our laughter. They said we were hilarious. By this time they were all aware of my dreadful shoe shopping experience with Jason. "Why are you purchasing two pairs of shoes in the exact same style and color?" "Well when I find comfortable shoes, I purchase two pairs. I keep the second pair as a spare when the first pair wears out."

"I am so glad you're doing this, I would have to hurt you if you asked me to come shoe shopping with you again."

"Now! I would suggest you replace your eyeglasses. The frames are too large and cover most of your face. The lenses are made of glass. They are thick and heavy, have you considered wearing contact lenses?"

"I am going to regret asking you for your help aren't I?" he replied.

Completely ignoring him I went on. "I will cut your hair in a style that flatters your features." "Okay, wait just one minute Noreen, I know you think bald men are sexy, but please do not shave me bald. I happen to like having all my hair." "No problem my friend," I smiled. "Put your head and trust in my hands."

"It makes me nervous when a woman asks me to trust her. The last time I did, it was not a pretty sight."

With a smile on my face, I said, "Yeah and she was probably a blonde too, wasn't she?" He smiled and turned his face away from me.

I cut and styled his hair, highlighting his facial features. "What a difference a good haircut makes, don't you think so, Jason?" "How would I know? I haven't seen it yet?" I handed him a mirror.

"Well, what's the verdict?" He looked shocked when he glanced in the mirror.

"I can't believe the change a good haircut makes. It looks great. How much do I owe you?"

I laughed, "Don't worry you will pay for this some way or another." He grunted. "Yes, I know and that's what scares me," while winking at me.

Previously he had no interest in how he dressed and looked and it showed. He went from dressing like a computer geek to a man dressed in stylish clothes.

"You need to dump the London Fog overcoat you wear. It is always wrinkled and way too big for you. We need to find you one that fits you well."

I could not help myself, I started laughing. He looked at me puzzled. "What's so funny?"

When I was able to compose myself enough to answer, I said. "The girls in the group say you look like Colombo wearing that overcoat."

"I happen to be fairly attached to my overcoat. I've had it for a long time. It still has life left in it. Besides, it's very comfortable."

"The overcoat has to go," I sighed. "Say goodbye to your coat."

The Saint Joseph's singles group was hosting a Valentine's Day dance a week prior to February 14th. Most of our group members signed up to attend the dance. None of the members had seen Jason after his transformation. I knew they would be startled at the change in his appearance. It was now Friday night and I had only one more night to contain my excitement.

"Jason, for the dance tomorrow you should wear your new black shirt and black jeans." He had already decided this was what he was going to wear. He however decided to be annoying.

"Why do I need to dress the way you want me to?"

Unhappily I responded. "Fine, wear whatever you wish. I felt the black shirt against your pale skin would make you stand out and the jeans accents your bottom well." He laughed, "I'm only teasing. I planned to wear these anyway. I'm only giving you a hard time."

I growled at him. "I can never tell if you are serious or joking. Your dry sense of humor can be annoying." He laughed again, "Don't lie you love it. Your life would be boring if I wasn't in it."

I smiled at him without responding.

The night of the Valentine's dance was finally here. I could barely contain my excitement. It was time for Jason to pick me up for the dance; however, he was late. This concerned me as he was never late for anything. I hoped there was nothing seriously wrong. He finally showed up 30 minutes late. Even though this put a damper on my excitement, I was happy to see him safe with no broken bones. He looked very handsome but appeared to be frazzled.

"I am so sorry for being late. I had a difficult time getting my contacts in. I almost gave up on them and wore my eyeglasses. I know how much you were looking forward to arriving at the dance early."

I responded with a bright smile. "No problem, I am just glad you are okay. You look handsome. Your black shirt and jeans look great on you."

"You don't look so bad yourself," he smiled back at me.

"Thanks."

I had difficulty pulling my dress zipper all the way up. It appeared to be stuck.

"Jason, could you please help me with my dress zipper? I can't get it all the way up?"

I turned my back toward him. Joshua, my older son, overheard the conversation and chimed in.

"Here Mom, let me help you with that."

Jason stepped back smiling knowing fully well Joshua at nine years old thought of himself as the man of the house. Joshua tried several times but could not get the zipper to budge. He turned to Jason.

"Here why don't you give it a try?"

Jason struggled but succeeded in finally getting the zipper up. As soon as the boys were picked up by their dad, we left for the dance.

The dance was being held in the school gymnasium. As we entered I looked around the room. I was hoping to get a glimpse of the group members. I was in luck as the first person I saw was Ricky. He was on the dance floor doing the tootsie roll.

"Hey, there's Ricky," I called out over the music. "As you can see, he rarely has a problem finding a dance partner."

It was not difficult to spot Ricky. He was 6'6", skinny, very handsome, and the life of the party. Ricky saw me and pointed me towards the table where the rest of the group members were seated. After dodging around the dancers we finally found our friends. Most of our friends didn't recognize Jason right away. They were amazed at his transformation. The girls who wouldn't give him the time of day before now wanted to dance with him. He was beaming at all the attention he was getting. He looked back at me and I smiled approvingly. He appeared self-confident yet humble with all the attention he was now receiving.

We were having a great time at the dance. Suddenly, Jason grabbed my arm and pulled me toward him. My heart skipped a beat thinking he was going to kiss me. Instead, he said.

"The contact I was having problems with earlier this evening, well it popped out of my eye making it difficult for me to see clearly."

With the dance hall being fairly dark there was no hope of finding his contact lens. If we did, it would have been flattened by the dancers' shoes. We stayed and visited with our friends a little longer and then said our goodbyes.

I depended on Jason's help in organizing several group activities. Being an engineer, he was always handy to have around. He was able to fix just about anything that was broken. He was a very honest person and if he gave you his word he would honor it.

To my excitement, one day Jason announced it was time for him to become a member of the group.

Jason helped me with the group potluck dinners held at my home. He had a calming effect on me. I was always stressed on the night of the potluck dinners. Jason said "Please leave me to worry about getting the dinner ready on time. You need to do what you do best, talk and entertain the guests as they arrive."

I thought it odd; Jason seemed to be too comfortable in the kitchen and was enjoying his role as Chef. He had things in the kitchen under control. I smiled to myself as I watched Jason in the kitchen wearing my red printed apron. I admired how calm he was while cooking the dinner. The paper plates were stacked neatly on one end of the countertop; the napkins and plastic silverware lay beside the plates.

I said. "Jason, if I was cooking for tonight's dinner I'd be a nervous wreck. There would be food splattered all over the stove. Is this the reason you motioned me out of the kitchen every time I came in?" Jason laughed saying, "I am saving you that embarrassment."

Once the potluck dinner was over, Jason started cleaning up the kitchen. He loaded all the dirty plates, napkins, and plastic silverware in large trash bags. He glanced around the house, making sure he didn't miss anything. He gathered all the trash bags and took them outside with him.

I thought it strange, Jason was enjoying being in the kitchen and cleaning way too much. I quickly dismissed this thought from my mind. I knew Jason was shy, and being in the kitchen kept him in the background.

In retrospect, I realized this was an important clue I should have had more concern about.

Most of the group members attended mass on Sunday mornings. We usually sat together as a group in the same church pew during mass. After mass we met at a restaurant for brunch. I always wondered why Jason did not attend church on Sundays. I excused this behavior thinking he just wanted to sleep in late.

At one of our monthly meetings, Chad, a recently divorced member of the group asked Jason, "Hey man, why don't you meet us at mass this Sunday? After mass, we will be going to brunch at the new little café down the street. Everyone says it is the best new café in town." Jason smiled, "I'm not sure if I will be at mass, I will definitely try to meet the group for brunch." This conversation was soon forgotten as the agenda for that evening's meeting was passed around the table. The meeting began with me leading the group.

The following Sunday after mass, the group headed to their cars and drove to the little café down the street for brunch. When we got to the café the owner, Oscar, greeted us. The group members recognized him as an inactive member of the group for the past two years. Oscar was glad to see everybody again. He personally escorted us to a table large enough to seat all of us. There was room to add more chairs if necessary. I was introduced to Oscar. He pulled out a chair for me and waited till I sat down.

Oscar was a dark-skinned, handsome man around 5'9". His body was muscular and toned. He seemed to take an interest in me. He said, "I moved from Columbia to Dallas seventeen years ago on a job offer. I was later sponsored by my company to become a US citizen. I stayed with the company for fifteen years. Two years ago, I decided to start my own business." I gathered from the sequels from the women, Oscar had a lot of admirers.

I gazed around the café which was not overly decorated. It didn't have all the bells and whistles like other surrounding restaurants. The dining area and the bathrooms were very clean.

Once everybody was seated, the server came over to take drink orders. Most of the women ordered sweet iced tea, the men ordered the café's house beer. The beer was claimed to be the best beer in town.

To everyone's surprise, Jason joined the group for brunch. He sat by me and my heart skipped a beat. As Jason was getting comfortable in his seat, Oscar came to the table with a drink. He said, "For the beautiful lady" deliberately speaking in a thick Columbian accent. It was a cool iced drink made of tequila and coconut milk.

Jason said, "Hey Noreen, how do you know, that drink is for you and not me?"

"Jason, he said for a beautiful lady, I am the only lady sitting between you and Chad." In retrospect I realized Jason was trying to give me a hint which I did not catch.

Chad asked Jason, "How come you didn't make it to mass, did you sleep in?"

Jason replied, "No I didn't sleep in."

Chad was not about to let this drop, "Then why were you not at mass?"

Jason now irritated responded, "I guess my earlier response didn't satisfy you. I am not Catholic, I am Methodist that's why I do not attend mass."

There was a pin-drop silence. It seemed to last forever. I broke out in laughter. The rest of the members joined in except Chad who looked confused. Once the laughter stopped I said, "Hey we are a Catholic singles group. How did you manage to squeeze in without any of us knowing you were Methodist?"

Jason just smiled and responded very quietly in my ear, "You will never know." This time my heart skipped a beat of foreboding.

As they were leaving the café, Oscar walked over to me, "Thank you for coming. I hope to see you again, right?"

I smiled at him and said, "The food was delicious and the service was excellent."

Falling in Love

Since we were spending so much time together, it was no surprise we fell in love. I was a short petite woman who didn't quite make it to five feet. My skin color was a deep tan with short brown hair. I was the complete opposite to what Jason thought he was looking for in a woman.

I jokingly asked him. "Should I wear a blonde wig to be the blonde bombshell you were hoping to fall in love with?" He responded: "That won't be necessary, I love you just the way you are."

Falling in love so soon after my divorce scared me. I remembered how unhappy I was in that relationship. I questioned whether it was too soon to be in a committed relationship. I knew he loved the boys. The thought of leaving them alone with him scared me. Crazy thoughts raced through my mind, "What if he was a child molester? What if he physically abused the boys when I wasn't around?"

To ease my mind I decided to test him. On several occasions I would leave the boys home alone with him. "Hon, I have some errands to run. Do you mind watching the boys until I get back? I shouldn't be gone more than an hour or so." He usually responded. "Take your time, dear, we three boys will have a good time together." When I did get home he and the boys were busy playing a game or on the computer. They were unaware I was even home.

I knew breaking the news of our love could alarm some friends in the group. We agreed not to say anything just yet. I was happy at how successful we were at keeping this a secret.

My potluck dinners were usually a huge success. This weekend was no exception. There was a higher turnout of female members at my potlucks. A very few attended the dinner events at restaurants. Most of the women like me were single moms with limited earnings. Knowing how costly childcare was, I always made it a point to invite their kids too.

My feet were extremely tired from standing all evening. I kicked off my high-heeled shoes. With a glass of wine in hand I plopped down in a sitting position on my newly carpeted living room floor, my back securely resting against the lower front edge of my Queen Anne-style couch. I was joined by my friend who seemed to have the same idea. We engaged in a serious conversation.

I was unaware Jason made his way to the couch sitting behind me. I was startled when he wrapped his legs around the sides of my body. This upset me. Only an hour before our first guest arrived we went over the pact we both made.

"Remember our agreement, no display of affection in front of the other members of the group."

This was yet another clue I missed. He would not respect our agreements going forward.

Heather rudely asked: "Since when has this been going on?"

Heather was an engineer. She did not participate in group activities very often. She had a negative personality. This made it difficult for others to be around her. I knew something had to be said since Jason was not responding. He just sat there smiling. I told our friends. "Jason and I are officially dating."

Nosey Chad laughed so hard his belly shook.

"Since you have him dressing sharp and looking good you decided to date him right? You had no interest in him when he dressed like a computer geek."

I laughed. "You're wrong, I was interested in him the first day we met last year in October at the pizza place. Look at him. Wouldn't you agree my hard work paid off?"

My friends from work, who had earlier met Jason, were surprised at his transformation too. They were aware of the seriousness of my relationship with him. They were already picking out bridesmaid's dresses from a bridal catalog they had in the office. I tried to stop this by reminding them he had not yet asked me to marry him.

Jason unexpectedly came by the office to invite me to lunch. My office door was open and faced the main entrance door to the suite. There was no time to hide the bridal magazine. He caught my friends flipping through the magazine in my office.

"I see you all looking through a bridal magazine, which one of you is getting married?" He grinned.

They smiled at him saying. "We are just looking as you never know, one of us may need ideas for our wedding. All we would then need is a wedding proposal from a very nice guy." Their eyes turned towards me. I was so embarrassed. Finally, I turned to Jason and said. I accept your lunch invitation, Jason. Can we please leave now?" At this point, I was head over heels in love with him and was extremely happy.

While at lunch I mused. "I can't imagine anything ruining the love we have for each other. Do you?" He did not respond. This was also a huge clue I missed.

When I returned to the office after lunch there was a huge bouquet of yellow roses sitting on my desk. My friends followed me into my office singing. "Here comes the bride."

The guys in the office also gathered in my office. They had heard all the commotion and came to see what was going on. They saw me sitting at my desk blushing with the bouquet of roses in front of me.

REALLY?

One night while we were on the couch talking, Jason suddenly became extremely serious. I had never seen him this serious before. He was always happy and had a dry sense of humor. "Honey, there is something I need to tell you." he began. Concerned, I sat up on the couch.

"I do not know how to tell you this without just being direct," he said. "You need to know I am a heterosexual crossdresser."

Being the naïve person I am, I said, "I do not understand what that means."

He tried to explain as simply as he could, "Honey, it means I enjoy wearing women's clothes, makeup, and shoes. I do not plan to have the surgery to become a woman. I am very fond of my boy parts."

I was now shocked. I did not know what to say. "How old were you when you first discovered you had the desire to dress as a woman?"

"I can remember back when I was five years old knowing I was different. I enjoyed playing with girly stuff while the other boys played with trucks and cars. When I was in middle school, I wore my mother's discarded pantyhose from her bathroom trash can. In high school, I was experimenting with my mother's clothes and shoes when she was not home. By the time I was in college, I was sharing a room with another guy. I didn't get to dress much except for wearing women's panties. After graduation, I left home to start a new job in another state. I started purchasing women's clothes and shoes online. I didn't have the courage to shop in department stores."

It seemed as though it was a relief for him to finally make the disclosure to me.

"From childhood, I always felt different from the other kids," he went on. "These feelings led me to believe I was a disappointment to my parents. I tried hard to please my mother more than my father. We lived on a farm and I suffered from severe allergies which kept me indoors most of the time. To make things worse, I didn't have friends. The only other person close to me was my mother. I found myself taking an interest in her activities, which developed my feminine behaviors. I learned how to cook, bake, and sew."

I was stunned. Total disbelief at hearing everything he was saying. My mind was so overwhelmed, it felt like I was waking up from a bad nightmare. I jumped off the couch and moved as far away as I could from him. I started to feel repulsed, betrayed, and sick to my stomach. I wanted to hit him. I felt dirty and wanted to tell him to leave right now. There were so many thoughts racing through my mind.

I thought about my two young sons who loved him. How would they react if he was gone? How would our church family feel about this? Would our church ask us to leave and find another church home? How would our families feel after hearing this? I contemplated breaking off our relationship. However, I loved him for his heart and kindness and not for the way he dressed.

His voice seemed very faint and distressed, "Noreen, please say something. I am so sorry. I did not mean to hurt you. I love you very much. I felt you needed to know before we proceeded any further in our relationship."

Now in tears and barely able to speak, I wanted it all to be a joke. A cruel joke, but not true at least. "Why didn't you tell me this when we met? Why did you wait till I fell in love with you?"

"I could not tell you this earlier," he responded. "I had no idea where our relationship was headed. When I did, I tried several times but panicked when an opportunity came up. I was afraid of losing you. I wanted to be sure you loved me completely too. I couldn't tell every girl I dated about my crossdressing. I couldn't trust them to keep this a secret."

I had so many questions that needed answers. "Does this mean I will be labeled as a lesbian whenever we go out with you dressed as a woman? My attraction toward you is specific to you, not an entire gender. I didn't choose this label. It is being forced upon me by you if I choose to remain in our relationship."

"Yes dear, we would be considered a lesbian couple," he replied.

I knew what I was hearing wasn't normal. It filled me with rage. I was mad at myself. Why didn't I pay more attention to the earlier signs of his characteristics being so feminine? Finally, I had to ask, "Are you gay?"

He grunted, "No, dear, I am not gay?" "Do you dress as a woman to increase your sexual pleasure?"

"No, honey, this has nothing to do with sex. You satisfy my sexual desires."

I reflected on my own religious beliefs on traditional marriage and the meaning of love and intimacy. After I recovered from the shock of his disclosure, I realized how much I loved him. I felt sorry for him. I knew how difficult it must have been for him to keep such a secret. He hadn't been able to discuss this with his family or friends for all these years.

I was still extremely angry. I asked him if I could see him dressed with women's lingerie. He agreed. We drove to his house and he ushered me into his closet. There were boxes of women's clothes and shoes he had purchased online. He picked out the lingerie. He proceeded to the bathroom to change. When he was done changing, he walked back into his closet. "What do you think honey?" Initially, I was repulsed and suppressed the urge to throw up. I made fun of the way he looked. I was extremely mean to him.

Finally, after all this sank in, I arrived at a place of acceptance. I ultimately fully accepted him for who he was. I didn't understand his need to be a crossdresser but decided to be receptive toward his needs. However, I told him all the clothes and shoes must go. The clothes and shoes in the boxes were not what a regular female would wear. Maybe a hooker might wear them however, I had my doubts.

I began to question my own sexuality.

My past life experiences were an open book. This helped me minister to other women. They came to me for advice on domestic violence. I always shared with them my life experiences, and my love for the Lord who I have always felt was near me, especially through difficult times in my life. As a believer, I am confident of being covered and protected by Christ's shield which surrounds me and which no human can break.

Jason's major secret now became mine too. This caused me fear, anxiety, and knots in my stomach. It made me physically ill whenever I was around friends and family. I couldn't speak to anyone about this skeleton that just came out of his closet. His coming out of the closet to me and put me in the closet with him.

I didn't realize how much his secret would affect my future life with him. How could I talk to my family about this? My only option was to isolate myself from my family and friends.

The Bells are Ringing

Our relationship and love for each other grew stronger over the years. One sunny afternoon in April, Jason invited me over to his home for lunch. He told me it was to meet his college roommate James and his wife Sarah.

To my surprise after lunch, Jason got down on one knee and proposed to me.

"Noreen, I love you and would like nothing better than to share my life with you. Will you marry me?"

Jason's crossdressing overshadowed my excitement. However, I responded with love.

"Yes, honey, I will marry you."

We picked a date for our wedding which gave me only four months to make preparations. I was quite nervous.

I could not help but compare Jason to my ex-husband. I realized there was no comparison. Jason was the gentlest soul I had ever met in my life. He was kind, caring, and loving to me and my boys. He didn't drink alcohol, smoke, or raise his voice at me or the boys. I sighed, this was the first time in my adult life I loved a man so deeply and completely. I was happy knowing he felt the same way about me.

He telephoned his parents to inform them of our upcoming marriage. He wanted to be sure they kept that date free. His parents lived out of town and I had not yet met them. He had already met my family and he seemed to like them.

As part of the wedding preparations, we had to decide on a church we would like to be married in. Jason felt since I was Catholic we ought to be married in my church. We made an appointment with my parish priest to learn more about the church's requirements for marriage.

We patiently sat in the church office waiting on Father Jerry Jackson to see us. Father Jerry came out of the church office and greeted us. He led us to his private office and asked us to be seated.

"So how can I help you?"

"Father, Jason and I are in love and we would like to be married in the Catholic Church," I said. "What are the church's requirements?"

"Noreen, since you are a divorcee, you will need to get an annulment. Jason you are not Catholic, therefore, you will need to convert to Catholicism. An annulment takes at least two years to process. You and Noreen have to wait two years before you can be married in the church. The cost for an annulment is a thousand dollars."

"Father, Jason is willing to become a Catholic," I said. "However, I can't afford the cost of an annulment. I have just got through paying for my divorce. Is there any way the Church can help me with the annulment costs?"

"The Church can't help you with this as we have our own overhead and attorney costs we must pay," said Father Jerry. I didn't believe in the need for an annulment, however, I decided to keep an open mind.

" Father Jerry, could you please explain to us what an annulment means?" I asked. "I have some idea however want to be sure my understanding is correct." Father Jerry did his best to explain.

"An annulment is a legal procedure which cancels a marriage between a man and a woman. Annulling a marriage is as though it is completely erased — legally. It declares that the marriage never technically existed and was never valid. "Noreen, the reason for your annulment is that you were not spiritually married to your ex-husband."

"Father, I can't use this reasoning. I knew exactly what was happening when I walked down the aisle with my ex-husband. I have given birth to two sons which proves to me a marriage existed. If our marriage didn't exist what would that make my boys?" Father Jerry knew exactly what I was asking, however, he refused to answer the question. "You are not Catholic," he said turning to Jason. "Therefore, you should not receive communion. At communion time, you can go up with everybody else and place your right hand or both hands forming an 'X' against your chest when you approach the priest. This is a sign that you wish to receive a blessing rather than communion. Anybody is welcome to receive a blessing, whether they are Catholics or not."

Jason pulled me aside.

"Noreen, we cannot wait two years for an annulment to come through," he said. "We have two young boys at home. We do not want them to see us living together for two years without being married."

I agreed with Jason.

By this time I was annoyed.

"Father, Jason is a member of the United Methodist Church. I am welcome to receive communion there. Unlike the Catholic Church, they do not refuse any Christians from partaking in communion."

I left our meeting with Father Jerry feeling totally disappointed.

In the car, I turned to Jason. "I would like to be married in the United Methodist Church where you are a member. We can both receive communion including the boys. This is important to me." Jason agreed. He hated to see me so discouraged and disappointed.

I called the United Methodist church the next morning and was given a time to meet the senior pastor that same day. I was thrilled and called Jason at work.

"Honey, we have an appointment this afternoon to meet your senior pastor. Can you get off work a little earlier today and pick me up? I would prefer we took one car." "Consider it done," he responded.

I was completely lost when we entered the Methodist church. Jason seemed to find his way around well. He kept tugging at my arm to steer me in the right direction. We were now sitting in an office waiting. An attractive casually-dressed lady walked in.

"We have an appointment with the senior pastor," I said. "We were asked to sit here and wait for him. If this is your office, we could always wait in the hallway."

She immediately started to smile. I looked at Jason. He was grinning from ear to ear. I could tell he was struggling to keep a straight face without breaking out in laughter.

I thought to myself, "Am I missing something? I didn't think I'd said anything funny so why are they smiling? This must be a Methodist thing."

"My name is Noreen and this is Jason. We are here to find out what the requirements are to be married in the Methodist church. I am Catholic and very nervous right now. I haven't been in a Methodist Church before, this is my first time."

I suddenly realized I hadn't given the lady an opportunity to speak. Smiling at me now she said, "I am the Senior Pastor. Your appointment is with me. I will be presiding over your marriage ceremony."

I was in shock, thinking, "I am such an idiot. Why didn't I pay more attention to the pictures on the wall with the captions saying she was the senior pastor?" I realized now why she was smiling and why Jason was grinning. He knew she was the senior pastor and failed to tell me.

"This is quite different for me. In my church only male priests performed wedding ceremonies."

"Would you prefer a male pastor?" she responded.

"I am comfortable with you performing the marriage ceremony," I said quickly.

We spent time talking and learning more about the church and the requirements needed for marriage in the Methodist Church. I was very impressed with the senior pastor's knowledge of the bible and her love for the Lord. I now felt completely at ease. One of the requirements of the church was that we attend pre-marital classes which we did. After one of these classes, we selected the music to be sung at our marriage ceremony.

I asked Maureen, a friend and coworker to be my maid of honor. My two bridesmaids were my niece and my coworker Juliet. The flower girls, Jasmine and Diana were sisters and the same age as my sons. They were to be escorted by my two sons, nine-year-old Joshua and seven-year-old Jude. Jason picked his friend, Joe, to be the best man. The two groomsmen were his college roommate James and his brother.

My wedding bouquet and all the flower arrangements would be a gift from a coworker and friend Juliet. I requested cream ribbons adorn all her flower arrangements. Since this was my second marriage, I refused to wear white, therefore, I wore a cream wedding dress and veil. Jason wore a long-tailed cream tuxedo jacket with black tuxedo pants. This was Jason's first marriage. Therefore I wanted him to be involved in every aspect of the planning.

A month before the wedding, the reception hall called me. They were confirming the date and time for the cake tasting.

"Would you like to go along with me for the cake tasting?" I asked Jason and was surprised at how happily he agreed. "I would love to."

As soon as we arrived at the place, we were greeted by the banquet hall manager.

"We have put together samples of our most popular cakes for you to taste," he said. We tasted three or four samples by which time my taste buds were overwhelmed. I didn't want to taste the remaining cake samples, knowing I wouldn't be able to tell the difference.

"Honey, I would like you to select our wedding and groom's cakes," I told Jason.

"Are you sure?" he asked.

I nodded in agreement.

He quickly responded, "Would you like to taste my final selection before we seal the deal or forever hold your peace?"

I laughed. "I trust your selection." (I am not a big fan of cakes. He was most definitely a cake lover.) He finally picked the cakes and knew I would love them too. A decision was finally made after he tasted five more samples of cake.

He carefully selected the design, taste, color, and intricate pattern for the icing on our cake. I was glad he made the decision. I was tired, cranky, and just wanted to go home.

I had a light bulb moment. Jason's mannerisms and behavior since I had met him started to make sense now. He wore my red printed apron in the kitchen at our potluck dinners. He was too picky in selecting the pattern and color of the icing on the cake. The comment at the restaurant when Oscar brought me a drink. The feminine way he put on and took off his eyeglasses.

Finally, the wedding day was here. Our families and friends arrived at the church. I began to get a little nervous. My bridesmaids were there to help me with whatever I needed. They reassured me things would be fine. I have a type "A" personality and just couldn't relax.

I heard my mom's voice down the hallway leading to the bride's room. As she got closer to the bride's room, I heard her say, "She is still my daughter. I need to give her my blessings before she walks down the aisle to be married."

I figured someone tried to keep her away prior to the ceremony. I was happy to see my mom and appreciated her blessings.

While I walked down the aisle I saw my young boys Joshua and Jude. I smiled to myself when I saw them in their little black tuxedos and Jason waiting for me by the senior pastor. The love I had for him poured out of my heart. I saw our friends from the singles group. They were smiling at me. Our friends were happy even though they were sad to see us leave the group. The music we selected for the service was beautifully sung by one of the church members.

The photographer was done taking pictures of the bridal party and our families. Jason, myself, and the boys left the church for the reception hall. We packed ourselves into a red sports car with the top down. The boys piled in the back seat, which was spacious enough for them. I took the passenger seat and Jason did the driving. My wedding gown was flying all over the place. It hit Jason in the face several times obstructing his view of the road ahead. Other cars passing us were honking and waving at us.

While driving Jason looked over at me. "Joe called me this morning laughing and asking. 'How are you holding up?' 'How do you think I'm holding up man, I am extremely nervous?' Joe hung up and before I knew it he and James were at the front door, ringing the doorbell. Joe said, 'We have the perfect remedy for your nervousness.' The three of us piled into James' car. We drove to a nearby bar. Joe knew the bartender, he was one of his friends. He told him 'My friend here is getting married in a couple of hours. Please fix him a fairly strong drink to get rid of his nervousness. Not too strong causing him to get smashed and out of control. His wife-to-be is also a friend of mine. She will never forgive me.'"

"We left the bar and headed straight for the church," Jason went on with his story. "When you saw me standing by the pastor, I was not only a bit tipsy, I was partially blind from wearing only one contact. I was running late this morning, I gave up trying to get the second contact in."

"I'm never surprised by what those two come up with," I laughed. "I'm surprised how easy it was for them to talk you into going to a bar at 10:00 a.m. You never drink alcohol."

"I needed something to calm my nerves and the alcohol did it."

Now grinning he continued with his story. "Just before we entered the church, James filled my pockets with marbles. They were weighing me down. This could explain why I seemed to be off balance to you." "Why did he give you marbles?" I asked. "He figured I had lost my marbles for getting married," Jason laughed.

When the bridal party got to the reception hall, my older brother told me the DJ hadn't yet arrived. He did his best to keep the guests entertained. Judging from the comments received from guests, he did an excellent job. I felt a little sorry for him as he was close to using up all his good jokes.

After some tense moments, the DJ finally arrived. The families were excited, he was finally there. The families' relief wasn't even close to the bride's; I was extremely relieved. The DJ apologized for his delay saying his car broke down on the way to the reception hall. Fairly quickly with some help, the DJ had his equipment set up. The party began with food and dancing.

It was now time for us to leave the reception hall. We said our goodbyes to our families and guests. We were led out through an archway of hands formed by our guests. We were showered with rice as we made our way through the archway. I was relieved my boys were staying with Jason's parents in our home while we were gone.

We had not eaten any food at the reception except for sharing a piece of our wedding cake. It didn't occur to us to pack some food from the reception for the night at the hotel. At 1:00 am I started to get really hungry.

"Honey, I am so hungry I haven't eaten all day."

Jason being a loving and thoughtful husband immediately responded with "Let's get dressed and go to a restaurant that serves breakfast 24/7."

We got dressed and off we went to get something to eat. We laughed all the way to the restaurant and back.

Family Life

I knew Jason would make a great dad because of his nurturing nature. He had a tender heart and compassion for my boys. He quickly adapted to his new role as a parent. He took his parental responsibilities seriously.

The boys asked him, "Do we need to change our last name, to take your last name?"

He responded. "You already have a dad, therefore, you don't need to take my last name. I do not need you taking my last name to prove you are my kids; you already are."

"What should we call you?"

He replied. "You can call me Jason."

Jason's parents lived in a very small country town in another state. They were extremely kind to their new family and asked the boys to call them Grandma and Grandpa. The boys were excited to have young grandparents they could do things with. Grandma always planned fun activities she knew the boys would enjoy on family vacations to see them. Grandma baked chocolate chip cookies for the boys and they loved them. Grandpa took the blades off his tractor. He had the boys take turns sitting in front with him riding on the tractor. This was the highlight of their vacation with their grandparents.

We made the decision not to tell our young sons about Jason's crossdressing. We felt this may only confuse them and we couldn't take that risk. His parents were also unaware of his alternate life. We continued our married life as if everything was okay. Jason's crossdressing always overshadowed any excitement I felt in our marriage.

Our lives revolved around Jude and Joshua's activities. Sports, church youth programs, and social events. Jason was not a fan of sports or the outdoors. He suffered from severe allergies. However, this did not stop him from attending the boy's baseball and football practices and games. He just made sure to take plenty of allergy medication before he left home.

While we were at one of Joshua's football games, there was a sudden unexpected downpour of rain. Jason didn't like being in the rain. He grabbed the towel off the top of the ice cooler, put it over his head, and held it away from his face. He didn't want his eyeglasses to get water on them. I looked at him and laughed.

Once Joshua was home from the game and showered, we talked about the day.

"Joshua, did you see Jason from the field when it started raining?"

Joshua gave me a big grin saying, "Yep, I sure did, he had a bright pink towel over his head keeping the rain off his face. It was hard not to miss, Mom."

We both began laughing.

"Quit picking on me," Jason said. "At least I didn't get my hair and eyeglasses wet. I can't say the same for your mom. I was the one stuck later drying out her eyeglasses."

Jason helped the boys with their homework. They asked for help only when they struggled completing an assignment. He walked them through the problems and let them figure out the answers. This frustrated Jude as he always asked for help at bedtime. By this time he was already sleepy, tired and cried because Jason wouldn't give him the answers. Jason was not going to solve the problems for him and didn't let Jude's behavior bother him. Jude's emotional state did however get to me. I would whisper in Jason's ear to give Jude the answers so he could go to bed. He wouldn't. This ended up in an argument between us. This caused a rift in our marriage.

Jason took time off work to attend every parent-teacher conference with me. He also took Jude and Joshua to their doctor appointments.

I thought I was fine with him disciplining the boys. One night, however, he brought home his very angry twelve-year-old son Joshua from football practice. Jason got on Joshua's case about his bad sportsmanship behavior on the football field at practice. Whenever Joshua was mad at Jason, he took it out on me and this day was no exception.

I was sitting in the living room sorting dirty laundry when they came home. Joshua walked into the living room mad, picked up a stack of dirty laundry, and threw it at me hitting me in the face. Jason did not tolerate Joshua or Jude disrespecting me.

"I will not have you disrespecting your mother and my wife like you just did," Jason said. "I am going to lay you across my knees and spank you. You pick the day and time when you would like this to happen."

Joshua now in tears and extremely angry said. "Let's go ahead and get it over with right now."

Jason was sitting by me on the couch in our living room where I was still sorting dirty laundry. He had Joshua lay across his knees and spanked him twice. It broke my heart and the tears kept rolling down my cheeks. I hid my face from Joshua so he wouldn't see me crying.

He was very fair with the boys regarding the house rules. He first explained the rules and then the consequences. When they broke the rules, he disciplined them.

Over the years our sons grew extremely close to him and felt comfortable calling him "dad."

We lived in a suburban home located on the north side of Dallas. The boys were attending schools with an excellent academic reputation. Jason felt it was important to live in the same neighborhood until the boys were through high school. This would allow them to have the same friends growing up, an opportunity he was never given.

When he was very young, his dad worked for a company that required him to move every two years. Jason's dad was a hardworking plant manager. This had a profound effect on young Jason. He had to give up his friends every time they moved.

"I wish my parents had discussed the move with me prior to it actually happening," he says. "It would have been nice if they asked me how I felt about moving. This was a painful experience for me. I thought what's the point in making friends? I will have to leave them behind when we move again."

At this point, little Jason gave up trying to make friends. He pretty much kept his feelings to himself at home. He had no childhood friends or stories to share as an adult. In Louisiana, he made friends with a kid who lived in their neighborhood. The kid came over often to ask if Jason could play outside. He and the kid became good friends. His parents had no idea moving so often affected him so deeply.

His parents finally decided to move back to their hometown. They both had aging parents at home. Jason had to leave the only friend he made and move with his parents. Once the move was made, he pretty much kept to himself. This resulted in him not being able to easily make friends as an adult. He did not learn the social skills needed to make friends when he was younger.

A short time after we were married. I quit my job to stay home with the boys. I had over ten years invested in this company. Whenever I traveled on business, Joshua managed to get himself in trouble at school. At the age of 10, he spent a lot of time in the principal's office. I knew my son was crying out for attention.

Every morning I dropped the kids off to school. Once I got back I locked myself in my home office and was on my computer. I visited every job site I could find to post my resume. I was only looking for positions that allowed me the flexibility to work from home. These jobs offered a lower salary than what I was accustomed to making. I was not deterred by this. My concentration lay in finding a job. I knew any money I earned would definitely help in decreasing our negative financial situation. Because I was unemployed and not contributing to the family income, it was a huge burden on us financially. Jason became resentful. I had more time to spend with the boys than he did. The loss of my income did not sit well with him either. This caused another rift in our marriage. I too was affected by the loss of my income. This was something Jason failed to see. The first year I was unemployed I felt miserable and depressed. I had to constantly remind myself of the reason why I quit my job. With me being home, Joshua's behavior improved significantly. I knew it was a blessing from God. Joshua's visits to the principal's office came to an end.

One afternoon, I ran into my old girlfriend Sally unexpectedly at a store. I had not seen Sally in years. We were both excited to see each other again and decided to have lunch that day. When Jason got home that evening I excitedly told him about the meeting.

"Jason, I ran into my old girlfriend Sally. We decided to have lunch. After lunch, I picked the boys up from school. The boys had no idea Sally had a pool and were very excited when they saw the pool. They enjoyed playing in the pool with Sally's son. Sally and I sat by the pool catching up on gossip."

Jason's response surprised me. "Must be nice, wish I had the time to sit by the pool."

Now I was irritated and said, "I thought we both agreed to this. I would quit my job and stay home with the boys. This allows me more time and interaction with the boys. Joshua's behavior and attitude have improved remarkably. The boys are always excited to see me in the carpool lane when school's out." I looked Jason square in the eyes. "Why have you been so hateful and resentful toward me lately?" I asked. I already knew the answer to the question. Jason wanted to play the role of the wife at home and I would never agree to this arrangement. This was yet another rift in the early stages of our marriage.

I applied for a sales representative position with a company and was hired. I worked a flexible schedule. I planned my customer visits around the boys' school schedules and activities. I had a list of assigned accounts in the DFW area. My job was to cultivate new business and grow existing accounts. After two years with the company, I heard the company was filing for bankruptcy. I decided to quit before this happened.

I went to real estate school to become a realtor. I received my Realtors' License and worked as a buyer's agent for three years. The real estate market started to decline so I put my license on "inactive" status.

Every evening Jason came home from work complaining. "The job is boring it doesn't challenge me at all." "Your complaining is stressing me out and making me sick," I finally said. "If you are unhappy with your job, start looking for another job before you quit this one."

One day unexpectedly Jason received a call from a job placement company. The company's client had a position open for a network administrator. They asked Jason if he was open to an interview with their client. Jason immediately said 'yes.' At the interview, he was offered the job. The company offered him a higher salary than what he was currently earning. He accepted the offer.

This made it his second job since we were married. He worked there for a little over 3 years. His constant complaining about the job started again.

One evening he came home from work.

"How was your day at work, Hon?" I asked.

He smiled. "At lunch today I put my feet on my desk and took a brief nap. My boss walked into the computer room along with his boss. I woke up but left my feet on the desk."

Horrified I said, "Jason, why didn't you go to the break room? You do know you could be fired for this."

"That would be great," he responded. "I won't be invited to attend any more meetings. They are boring and I fall asleep at them."

I was shocked at his selfishness. He didn't even give a second thought to his family's financial stress if he had been fired. Jason was an extremely intelligent man with a gifted brain. He however lacked common sense.

"Noreen, you worry too much, you need to knock it off. You are always being negative towards me and never support me. You always take the company's side."

I started to get irritated and frustrated with Jason. I was about to start an argument with him but decided against it. Any discussions we have had so far ended up with Jason feeling he was right and I was wrong. The stress of listening to him complain all the time started to wear on me. I craved financial security in my marriage. Unfortunately, I knew Jason was not the man who could give it to me.

I have now started to work for another company as an account executive. I worked out of my home office. This week I traveled out of town for a company sales meeting. I was surprised when my phone rang early one morning. It was Jason. We usually spoke to each other at night. Knowing something was wrong I became concerned.

"Where are you at?" I asked him.

"I'm at home," he responded.

"Did the company let you go?"

"Yes they did," he said. I laughed hysterically. It didn't take the company even a week to end his contract.

"I am glad you are taking it so well," he continued. "I had a hard time making this phone call to you. Thank you for making it easy on me."

The FBI is Interested in Us???

Jason was out of work again this time for almost a year. His obsession with cross-dressing began increasing. He had too much time on his hands.

He had applied for a job with a government contractor. He received a call for an interview. After the interview, he was called back with a job and salary offer. The salary offer was the most Jason had ever made in his career. We were both excited. This job would definitely help us solve our debt issues over time.

Jason and five other Systems Administrators were hired by the company. The projects they were hired to work on were delayed. The company decided to have the talent hired and in place anyway. The six of them were told to read up on company information and other technical literature in the meantime.

After about two weeks Jason was frustrated and angry at not having anything constructive to do. He was bored once again. He was annoyed the company was paying them a salary to do nothing. I begged him to be patient. I asked him to spend this time catching up on the new software and technology updates he so desperately needed. He became very angry and started throwing accusations at me. He was now on his soapbox with, "You are never on my side and you are always siding with the company."

I could feel myself tense up and anger building. I said. "I have never met anyone at this company either. I can't understand where this is coming from. I have no clue why you keep throwing accusations at me. I have some knowledge of what companies expect from their employees. I have been in the workforce for years longer than you have."

He got more heated when I tried to explain to him what acceptable behavior was and what wasn't. Unfortunately for our family, he always went with the unacceptable behavior. After this argument, he did not complain anymore.

One afternoon, I was lying on the couch in the living room. I had just taken a shower and put on PJs. I wasn't feeling that great. I figured I would rest before picking the kids up from school. The front door opened and I heard Jason's voice. I thought it strange that he was at the front door. He always drove through the back alley using the driveway into our garage. Then I heard his voice more clearly saying.

"Dear, I am not alone, there is someone with me." I sat up and saw a tall skinny man in a trench coat walk in with him. He introduced himself as an FBI Special Agent. I looked at Jason trying to figure out what was going on. He didn't respond to me and just had a blank look on his face.

The next thing I knew, there were a half dozen or more FBI agents wearing FBI vests walking into our home with guns drawn. I was stunned. "Please put your guns away, we do not allow guns in our home." They had some type of warrant in their hand to search the premises. I just got a glimpse of it when they flashed it in my face.

I was asked to take a seat on a chair in our formal dining room. Jason had to sit across the table from me. I repeatedly asked him. "What have you done?" He refused to respond. The FBI Special Agent with the trench coat started asking me questions about Jason. I was so confused my head was still reeling from them being there. The questions were directed only toward me. Jason just sat there stone-faced.

From where I was sitting, I could see the other agents headed upstairs. On the second floor was Jason's office and the boys' bedrooms. They came down the stairs with Jason's and each of the boys' computers. They also had files and disks belonging to Jason. I felt extremely violated as they went through each and every room in our home. They were grasping at straws, looking for anything that might incriminate Jason. At this point I wasn't sure who I was mad at more Jason or the FBI. I felt so violated by the agents going through our personal stuff.

Then a couple of agents who were in Jason's closet came out shaking their heads. They didn't have to say a word to me. I knew they had found the cross-dressing clothes, makeup and shoes in his closet.

It was now several hours later since our home was invaded by FBI agents. I was no closer to finding out why they were there than I was when they arrived. My frustration started to show and I became irritated with the FBI agents. "I am going to my bedroom to put on some makeup and to change clothes.

One of the female agents stood up and began to follow me to my own bedroom. She stood outside our bedroom leaving the door wide open so she could see me. I sarcastically asked her. "Are you going to stand there and watch me undress?" She nodded. "Yes ma'am, I need to make sure you don't pull a gun on us." I responded. "You've got to be kidding me." It was quite humiliating for me as I did not change in front of any woman staring me down.

While getting dressed I asked. "What did my husband do?" She didn't give me an answer either.

"My husband is a very honest man," I said. "He was once given fifty cents extra in change, he went back into the store and returned it to the clerk. I am not sure what you guys think you have on him, you have the wrong man."

I suddenly realized it was around 3:00 pm and the boys would be getting out of school. I called my friend Sally. "Sally, could you please pick up the boys from school and keep them at your house? I am not sure what time we will pick them up. We have the FBI agents here with their guns drawn. I do not want the boys to come home and see this. It may be traumatic for them. I will tell you what's going on later when I pick the boys up from your home."

Of course, Sally agreed. After about another hour or so, the agents collected a total of five computers and a bunch of files. They told us they were taking them to the FBI headquarters in Dallas. Once they were done with them we would get them back.

Once they left, I immediately called an attorney to represent Jason if they arrested him. I suddenly realized I still didn't even know what Jason had done. I had him speak to the attorney. The attorney told us the most that we can expect to happen, he would lose his job.

Finally Jason told me he was bored at work. He developed a software that could crack any password. Such a technology already existed however, he decided to write his own. He mentioned this to one of his co-workers who he believed turned him in. I didn't even bother to say another word to him. I couldn't believe how someone could be so intelligent and gifted yet lack common sense.

We finally stopped by Sally's house to pick up the boys. We talked to them for some time and left with the boys to go home. The boys showered and went to bed. They hadn't noticed their computers were missing.

Jason had worked for the National Security Agency (NSA) in Maryland. He was flown to the FBI Agency in Washington for questioning. They threw a lot of questions at him all at once. They were trying to determine if he was a spy. Apparently he didn't appreciate the attitude of the woman asking the questions. Therefore, he began to antagonize her which got her upset. She had him take a lie detector test, which he failed. He thought the questions being asked for the lie detector test were stupid.

Jason was very arrogant and ended up losing his job just as the attorney had said. We also lost the $6,000 we paid to the attorney as a retainer's fee. For at least two years later the FBI had our phones tapped listening in on our conversations. Five years later, we received our computers and files back. The computers were already obsolete by this time and were of no use to us. We ended up giving the computers away to single moms who couldn't afford a computer for their kids. Jason was kind enough to set up the computers for them in their home.

The FBI episode caused a major rift in our marriage. I didn't think our marriage could survive this. I was extremely upset and didn't realize how disappointed I was in my marriage to Jason.

Walking on Eggshells

I was walking on eggshells almost everywhere we went. Jason became so excited about his alternate life. I was afraid he would slip up and say something that would reveal our secret. The financial stress, the FBI incident, and the cross-dressing had a huge impact on my health, which was declining fast. My friends jokingly said. "Noreen, since you married Jason you are always sick. Are you sure you are not allergic to him?"

I dwelled on what my friends said. Even though I knew they were only joking. I questioned if there was some truth to it. I dismissed this thought right away. I thought to myself, "You all don't know him like I do." Very few husbands serve their wives a cup of tea in bed these days. Jason also had my pills sorted. He prepared my tea in my favorite red aluminum teapot that I loved dearly.

"I'm not sure what's happening to me. I've been sick throughout our marriage," I said flippantly. "It's probably related to stress. I can't imagine what else it could be?"

Jason did all the cooking in our house in addition to our laundry. The boys did their own laundry whenever they were home from school. Jason disliked folding clothes, he usually brought them to me to fold while I watched TV. This didn't bother me at all as I loved the warmth of the clothes against my skin as I folded them. Any time I stepped into the kitchen, Jason gently led me out.

"He is confident my illness is due to the change in my diet. He doesn't eat the type of foods I enjoy. This is one of the reasons he took over the cooking."

"What's his point?" Shelia asked. "He feels it's probably the bread, pasta, and starch he has introduced in my diet. I have become so dependent on him. There are times I can't even stand up on my own without his help. Very often he had to gently carry me off the couch and lay me on our bed."

We cashed in our retirement accounts to keep up with our monthly expenses. This time it took him almost two years to find his next job.

The new company offered him a decent salary with a one-year contract. His job was to automate the daily functions performed by employees. This allowed employees to use the time saved more efficiently on other functions needing attention. I worked hard to earn an income so I could help with the finances.

"You need to start looking for your next job before this one ends," I suggested to him once again. Of course, he didn't budge. He thought I was controlling every time I asked him to look for another job. The company extended his contract for an additional six months, but could not extend it any further. His contract ended. He didn't seem to care his family was suffering financially once again.

We decided to join a church that Jude was visiting with his friend. We visited for several months. I loved the support we received from the church. The boys tolerated the church's youth program. Keeping Jason's secret from our church friends was extremely difficult for me. Once again, Jason's inability to find work added to my stress level. The church members knew of our financial struggles. They had no idea he was a crossdresser.

Almost every evening when I came home from work, he was on the couch sleeping.

The continuous loss of his income put our family way behind on our financial commitments. This caused tremendous frustration for me. My frustration was exhibited in anger toward him. I knew he was not actively looking for a job even though we were suffering financially.

Jason, still unemployed, was absorbed by a company my brother and I created. From a technological aspect, he was a tremendous asset in growing our business, however, the company couldn't afford to pay him what he was worth. I begged him to look for another job as we were not meeting our financial commitments. He refused to look. My brother also had a talk with him.

"Man, we would love to have you. We just can't afford to pay you what you are worth. Your family is financially suffering."

He refused to find another job. I sold my company shares to my partner and opted out of the business. He continued working for the company. Finally, the company had to let him go as sales were down.

The pastor and deacons from the church knew of our difficulties. It was evident to them he was not seriously looking for work. By this time I lost all respect for him.

A deacon from the church visited our home. He spoke to Jason.

"Why is it taking you so long to find another job?" he asked. "Are you seriously looking for a job? What kind of a job do you hope to get? Several people from church have provided you with job leads, why haven't you pursued these leads?"

"I am looking for a job that allows me to work from home," Jason responded. "I want to have my own schedule and not be tied down to a 9-5 job."

"Everybody would like that too, Jason," the deacon responded. "You need to be willing to accept a job with any schedule. You have a family to support."

Not making any headway with him, he politely excused himself and left our home.

After two years of not working, Jason received a lead from a friend who was a member of the church.

"Our company is hiring and I have referred you for one of the positions," he said. He was called for an interview and was hired by the company. He and I praised and thanked the Lord for this blessing. After working there for almost three years, the company suffered a setback and he was laid off. The company started re-hiring the employees that were laid off. I was excited and was confident he would be re-hired.

My excitement lasted only a few minutes. He told me he and two other employees were exchanging chat messages. In the chat messages, they called their boss degrading names and made fun of him. When he was laid off his boss got his computer. He read all the chat messages he had sent out. Jason never deleted any files. The other two employees did. When his boss read the messages, he told the other two employees that he was debating on who to cut from the department.

"After reading these messages," he said, "I know my decision to let him go was the right one."

I decided to join a women's bible study at church. Many of the women shared their joys and struggles. I just sat there and listened. I could not come out openly and talk about Jason's crossdressing. I knew the pastor teaching our class would not be happy at hearing he was a crossdresser. Besides, I wasn't sure how the other women would feel if they knew this.

There were many days I drove home crying because the isolation was gripping my heart. I was afraid my friends would ask me to leave him. My family wouldn't want to hear or discuss this issue with me.

We were members of the church for almost five years. I heard a rumor that the deacons of the church may ask him to leave. They felt he was not living up to his role as the head of the household. He always argued with anybody who attempted to have a discussion with him on the subject. His response was always, "the bible doesn't say that only men needed to work nor does it say women shouldn't work."

I started to wonder if I was still in love with him. Wanting to spare him the embarrassment of the church asking him to leave, I made the decision to leave the church. He didn't know the real reason we were leaving. He agreed as he was not happy with the church either. I knew by changing churches, I would lose my church and the family and friends I had made there.

We had been visiting churches for several weeks prior to leaving our home church. We finally decided on joining the Methodist Church where we were married. The church had a large youth group. The youth program offered several activities our boys enjoyed while visiting. Joshua and Jude loved the youth worship service held on Sunday nights. We dropped the boys off at church on Sunday nights. Since we were already there we decided to volunteer in the kitchen preparing and serving meals to the youth.

Since I was not currently working, I signed up for a women's bible study at the new church. The study was held in the morning on weekdays. Jason and I joined a small group. The group met on Sunday mornings prior to the church service we attended. We were very happy with the new church and made several new friends. We loved our small group. I decided to join the church choir.

At church socials, instead of hanging out with the circle of men, Jason hung out with the women. I didn't feel like taking part in the conversations with the women as he was always in our circle. Most women like to have 'girl time' and I felt I couldn't since he hung out with us women. Several times I nudged him motioning him to join the men. I did realize with him being a crossdresser, he had more in common with women. However, with him dressed in guy mode at these socials, he stood out like a sore thumb.

The stress of keeping Jason's secret was wearing thin on me. I missed church often as I was always ill. I had discovered that I suffered from Fibromyalgia. This is thought to be the result of overactive nerves. It is a condition that results in chronic widespread pain and tenderness all over the body.

Over the years with all the stress, pain, and anxiety, I was physically ill almost every day. He knew I couldn't work outside the home anymore. The flare-ups and body aches were more noticeable whenever I was stressed.

I made friends easily in the Methodist Church. Our church group was very concerned about my health. They lifted me up in prayer whenever they didn't see me at church on Sunday mornings.

I was never relaxed nor at peace visiting anybody at the time. I wasn't sure what Jason would say next. He was getting bolder with his cross-dressing. I was afraid he would drop hints about his alternate life. I continued to isolate myself from family and friends.

One Sunday after service, I went looking for him. I found him talking to the guys in charge of the music and cameras. He was joking with one of them when I found him. As I got closer, I could hear him say, "I bet you would look good in a mini-skirt."

The guy laughed and took it as a joke. I felt my body get extremely cold and fear started to overcome me. He was breaking every agreement we set with regard to his cross-dressing at socials we both attended. Situations like this only increased my anxiety attacks. I had to confront him.

"Every time you speak to men about looking good in women's clothes it makes me extremely uncomfortable," I said.

But he was no longer concerned about my feelings.

"You've become so controlling, get over it," he responded like he usually did lately.

My symptoms got worse as time passed. "Noreen, your illness is related to stress and anxiety," my doctor said. "I would like to know what's going on in your life to cause this."

I could not bring myself to tell my doctor. "My stress is related to Jason being a crossdresser. Our financial situation is a disaster and not being financially secure has caused my health to decline."

What I didn't realize at the time was that Jason had already told our doctor about his cross-dressing. When I called him on this he didn't seem concerned.

"I had to tell him since my appointment was an annual physical. He would see my nipples pierced with rings on them."

"Having your nipples pierced is a fetish and has nothing to do with crossdressing. Dr. Brown has been my doctor for 25 years before I even knew you. It would have been nice if you had discussed this with me first."

"You worry too much. Get over it."

He rarely dressed as a woman during the boy's impressionable years. When he did, he restricted it to our bedroom. I loved and supported him. However, when it came to making love, the boundaries were set and made crystal clear to him.

"I need to make love to my husband and not you dressed as a woman," I told him. "There will be no wigs and women's clothes during this time. "Honey, I respect your feelings and I will honor them," he responded.

Over the years Jason did not honor my feelings. He constantly manipulated me into agreeing to the bras, panties, and high-heeled shoes in bed. This created a tremendous amount of stress and pressure on me. I didn't care anymore and agreed. This type of manipulation continued throughout our marriage. Our sex life became non-existent over the years as this was a turn-off for me.

I continued living with this huge black cloud over my head. My friends who knew me well had no idea what I was going through. How do you tell someone my husband likes wearing women's underwear in bed?

Take a Walk on the Wilder Side

There was a four-year age difference between Jason and me. I noticed as he was getting closer to his fiftieth birthday, his desire to crossdress increased. It became increasingly difficult for him to keep it a secret. He would sometimes slip up and say something to our friends without realizing it.

The years had flown by so fast. Joshua and Jude had left home to attend universities in different states. Since the boys had left home, I felt Jason needed to find an appropriate outlet to express his feminine side. I wanted him to learn more about why he had the need to cross-dress.

One day at dinner, I spoke to him. "You have put your feminine desires on the back burner for me and the kids all these years. I feel you need to find a group of heterosexual crossdressers like yourself. This group could become a source of support for you in understanding your need to cross-dress."

He could not believe how supportive I was about him being a crossdresser. He was so excited. He immediately got on the internet looking for groups in Dallas. I had no idea I had unleashed the beast in him. I felt he needed an outlet to express himself as a crossdresser. I was tired of being fearful every time we went out. I had no idea I would live to regret this decision.

He finally found a group of heterosexual crossdressers who were married to genetic women. He called the telephone number on the internet site and spoke to Rodney who was the president of the group.

He and Rodney communicated several times with each other through emails and phone calls before they actually met. They selected a date, time, and a meeting place.

He was filled with excitement and nervousness. I hadn't seen him this happy in a long time.

"I have set up a meeting date with Rodney and his wife Destiny. Rodney suggested I bring you along as your support is very important. Rodney has a few more questions for us and depending on our responses, he will give us more information. Rodney and Destiny are senior members of this group. What do you think? Will you go with me to meet them?"

"I hadn't planned on being involved with this group," I said. "I wanted you to have the opportunity of being with men whom you could relate to as a crossdresser."

"But you have been extremely supportive of me as a crossdresser, it would make me feel more comfortable if you came with me."

On the day of the meeting, he called Rodney to confirm the meeting was still on. We arrived at the meeting place earlier than expected. We waited for Rodney and Destiny to show up. Rodney gave Jason a vague description of himself and Destiny. Every couple that passed by we wondered could this be them? Finally and on time Rodney and Destiny approached us, looking a bit awkward.

"Are you Noreen and Jason?"

The introductions were made and general courtesies exchanged. Rodney asked Jason several specific questions about his cross-dressing. Rodney was satisfied with his answers. He now gave us some more information about the group.

"Our group is very selective in picking our new members," said Rodney. "The places we meet are always kept private. This allows us to protect the identities of all our members. Some of our members are CEO's and Presidents of companies. We also have doctors and surgeons attending our events. Therefore, we cannot afford to compromise their identities. If this happened, it would ruin their careers and most likely destroy their families."

Listening to Rodney speak I thought to myself *"Goodness gracious my life is going to change!"*

Jason was now signing the forms to become a member. He looked relaxed, happy and content. The forms were laid in front of me to sign. There were so many thoughts racing through my mind. The reality suddenly hit me. Smiling and giggling my thoughts were, "*WOW! We have just signed up to become members of the Crossdressers Witness Protection Group.*" I didn't share my strange thoughts with Jason, he wouldn't think it was funny.

I enjoyed talking to Destiny who was very friendly. We shared our funny experiences married to crossdressers.

"You guys should attend our social this weekend," said Rodney. This will give you the opportunity to meet the other members of the group in a social setting."

After meeting Rodney and Destiny, I took to them immediately.

"Where do we sign up to attend this event?" I asked. "We are so looking forward to meeting the rest of the group members."

Jason's jaw fell open and he chuckled to himself. He couldn't believe how excited I was for us to meet couples like us. Jason was absolutely thrilled once we left the meeting. When we were back in our car and headed home he was excited.

"I am finally going to meet men I can relate to, which makes me nervous and excited. You have such an outgoing personality you will make friends with the wives immediately." He hoped meeting wives in my situation would ease some of my stress.

At the meeting, Rodney had asked Jason to choose a feminine name. This name would be used by the other group members. This became especially important when attending group events. I had the option to change my name too if I felt it was necessary to protect my identity. I decided to stick with my own name. I had confessed to Rodney and Destiny that there were days when it was hard enough for me to remember my own name.

"Can you imagine what my pea brain would do to me if I took on an additional name?"

We had a full day with Rodney and Destiny. Once we got home Jason immediately went to get his laptop. He placed it on the breakfast table and sat down in front of it. The breakfast room overlooked the kitchen. He was on a mission to find the perfect feminine name to be used. He took a considerable amount of time online researching different female names.

I was in the kitchen preparing dinner. He began calling out names from a list he prepared. Thank goodness, he couldn't see me smiling with amusement. Being silly, I remember thinking, "Am I having a baby girl and nobody told me?" I could hear his voice in the background sounding a tad bit irritated.

"I need you to pay attention to the names, as your opinion on these names are important to me." In an attempt to be supportive, I offered my opinion on a few names he called out. Once again, reality smacked me in the face. It was unbelievable. Here I was helping my husband pick his feminine name. He continued to call out more names.

Now my patience was running extremely low and I had reached the point of being aggravated. I was cranky, tired, and hungry with a severe migraine. He kept on interrupting me from preparing dinner by asking my opinion again and again.

"I have already given you my opinion," finally I had enough. "Why are you still calling out names to me?" It finally dawned on me, it was obvious he didn't seem to care I had a severe migraine and we hadn't had dinner as yet.

"Good grief, Jason, just pick a name, how difficult could this be?"

He looked at me in anger. "I am picking a feminine name which is important to me. I wish you would quit being so insensitive."

That was the wrong thing to say to me at this time. I now lost it and couldn't control my anger anymore. The dam burst.

"I have been very sensitive to your need to be a crossdresser. How about paying more attention to the name Jason? The man I married. Do you even remember him? You have gone back to your old style of dressing as Jason. Your closet consists of faded polo shirts and a couple of pairs of pants you wear every day. Your shoes are old and have holes in them. However, you continue to wear them. You very rarely want to go out with me in guy mode. When we do go out, I am embarrassed by the way you dress as a man. You spend more money buying women's clothes than men's. When we are out shopping you head straight to the intimate section of the department store going through bras and panties. Your closet consists of more women's clothes. I have to go out and buy men's clothes for you which you may or may not wear. You have about 20 pairs of women's shoes and only one pair of men's shoes.

"When we receive an invitation to an event not relating to crossdressing you persistently ask me if you can go dressed as a woman. You know full well my answer will be no. The constant asking and pushing only irritates me. The more persistent you are the greater my stress level becomes. We always end up in an argument. This leaves me extremely frustrated and mentally drained. I feel like a mother reminding her child about our "Rules of Crossdressing."

He was shocked at my outburst and I was too. Until today he had no idea how strongly I felt about his crossdressing. The cross-dressing consumed his life and some days he forgot he had a wife.

"Look, Jason, you have become very self-absorbed, self-centered, and selfish. You have not taken my feelings into consideration."

"Honey, I am so sorry," finally he responded. "You are right. This is a sensitive time for you. Please understand your feelings are very important to me. I love you very much and will be more sensitive in the future."

As if the outburst had never taken place, he said, "I have selected the name, Faye Wilder. Honey, what is your opinion on this name?"

I gave him the thumbs up and continued preparing dinner. I didn't even bother to turn back and look at him.

The Crossdressers' Social Circle

The other woman in our marriage was Jason's feminine side, Faye Wilder. Faye always hid her jewelry and makeup in places where I couldn't find them. I am not sure why she did this. Her complexion was very pale and the jewelry she wore was not my style anyway. My complexion was a lot darker than Faye's. It took her two hours to get dressed for an event. Once she was dressed she ran around the house looking for her jewelry and makeup.

It was very sad to watch Jason becoming more female than male; I was gradually losing my husband to "the other woman," Faye.

I had an anxiety attack when we were about to leave for the event. Before leaving the house, I walked to the alley and looked to see if the coast was clear and that no neighbors were out. Once I was sure there were no neighbors out, I signaled Faye to pull out of the garage. I quickly jumped in the car and we drove off.

Faye got irritated with me as I was afraid of the neighbors seeing us.

"I do not care if our neighbors see me dressed as Faye," she said. "In fact, I am hoping they see me so you can quit being so scared."

I supported Faye in almost all her feminine changes. It was hard to believe Faye was willing to reveal her secret to the neighbors, compromising our family. I was scared for our neighbors to see Faye. I contemplated how I would respond to their questions. What would I say to them? How would I react if the subject of Faye came up? I felt there was no point expressing my feelings to Faye. She would get aggravated and tell me I was overreacting.

While driving to the event, Faye was giving me some pointers.

"When you speak to a crossdresser you always address the person as 'her' or 'she.' It is acceptable to address a crossdresser in guy mode as 'he' or 'his.' When I am dressed as a woman you need to remember to call to me Faye."

Going out shopping with Faye to pick an outfit for the event was very stressful. We received a few looks from people who recognized Faye as a man. Most people didn't even pay any attention to us.

I suggested a few age-appropriate outfits for Faye to consider. She had several reasons why she didn't want them. She was attracted to clothes that showed as much skin as she could get away with. She finally picked a revealing top, a very short mini skirt and high spiked heels. This of course did not meet my approval. I tried talking Faye into wearing something more modest, but she didn't want to have that conversation.

I insisted she wear an age-appropriate outfit for the evening. Destiny told me at our first meeting that most of the members wore age-appropriate outfits. I reminded Faye about this.

"You have a closet full of outfits," I said. "I'm sure you can find something to wear."

Dealing with Faye on the night we were to attend the group event was absolutely maddening. She acted like a spoilt seventeen-year-old daughter. She just invaded our closets, hogged the bathroom and required a lot of attention. Every few minutes she would interrupt my dressing asking me to help her with something she needed. This left me with not enough time to get dressed for the event. I was disappointed that Faye paid so much attention getting dressed as a woman and had no interest in how she looked dressed in guy mode.

As I had expected, Faye forgot where she hid her jewelry. She did such a great job of hiding them that even she couldn't remember where she hid them. This ended up in an argument.

"I know you found my jewelry and makeup. You moved them to another place while cleaning the house."

When she calmed down she remembered where she hid them. She apologized. "I'm sorry for blaming you. You know how nervous I get meeting new people. I love you very much."

I was so tired of Faye's arguments and her ending them with the apology, "I love you very much you do know that right?" This happened so often I was losing patience and interest in going out with Faye.

When we finally made it to the event, Rodney and Destiny were in the parking lot. They were getting stuff out of their car. When they were done, we walked along with them to the room reserved for this event. My initial reaction was shock seeing so many crossdressers in one room. Some of them were well put together, others definitely had room for improvement. You could tell very quickly the ones whose wives supported their crossdressers and the ones who didn't. They were usually absent or extremely uncomfortable at the events. Some of the crossdressers could have used help with their makeup and outfits.

This was our first time out in a group setting of this size. The event started with food and soft drinks. We mingled with the crossdressers and their wives. Everybody was extremely friendly which made us feel comfortable.

I had a hard time remembering to use "she" when speaking about another crossdresser. My instincts were to say "he." By the end of the night I was so confused. I kept calling people "he" or "she." The group immediately took to me as I did to them. One of the crossdressers jokingly corrected me when I said "his" instead of "her." They knew this was our first visit to the group. They were just happy I was there supporting my heterosexual cross-dresser spouse.

In several intense conversations with some of the crossdressers at the event, it was surprising to see how much in common each of their journeys had been.

"Growing up we were not allowed to dress in female clothing openly. Therefore, it is not unusual for some of us in our mid-forties and fifties wearing clothing designed for teenagers. Unfortunately, some of the overweight crossdressers also go this route. Their bodies are not designed to look graceful in these clothes. This ruins the image for the rest of us crossdressers."

I felt life should not be this complicated. The crossdressers spent years anticipating and planning their coming out. Whereas the "genetic" women married to them were not given the same opportunity. Most crossdressers come out of the closet between the ages of 30 to 50. They had suppressed their desire for years while raising kids and working to provide for their families. The majority of crossdressers I met worked in the computer industry or the engineering field.

After the social hour ended, several of the crossdressers began setting up chairs in a circle preparing for the next part of the event, which was an open discussion with a psychologist. Faye joined the crossdressers sitting directly across from the group of wives. She sat like a guy with her legs spread apart leaving nothing to the imagination. This did not go unnoticed by one of the wives sitting by me.

"Faye is sitting like a guy," she whispered in my ear, laughing. "I am going over to remind her to keep her legs together."

"Go ahead," I smiled back. "I noticed this too when I sat down."

She walked over to Faye and whispered in her ear.

"You are sitting like a guy, ladies keep their legs together especially when wearing a skirt."

Faye gave her an embarrassed look and quickly put her legs together.

The group met once a month. Faye came out of the house closet only to move into a larger closet where she expressed herself as Faye. My stress was replaced with happiness. After 10 years of marriage, I was able to be "ME," personality and all. I enjoyed attending the group events. The stress disappeared for one night a month. I didn't have to hide the skeleton for this one night.

Like Faye, I too felt excited. The skeleton I've carried for the past 10 years was finally out. I enjoyed speaking to women who had walked in my shoes for years.

Every month I looked forward to attending the events planned for the month. Looking at the crossdressers, I could tell most of them took pride in their appearances. Before we discovered this group, Jason and I usually dressed casually wherever we went. I longed to dress in pretty feminine clothes which I did for these events. Of course, it depended on how high-strung Faye was that night.

For this month's social, we were going to meet at our usual place and then head to the restaurant. I was surprised to see about fifteen couples attending.

When we got to the parking lot of the restaurant, I saw a crossdresser still sitting in her car. I remembered her from our first social. At the time, he was dressed in guy mode, and 'his' jokes were funny. He changed his feminine name twice. I wasn't sure what name she was going by now. The last I heard she was going by the name of Michelle. I went over to her car.

"Hey Michelle, what are you still doing sitting in your car? Come on out and walk with us to the restaurant."

I waited till she got out of her car. We started walking toward the entrance of the restaurant talking to each other. I held her hand remembering now that it was very cold, but I didn't think much of it.

We were busy talking as we walked together toward the entrance of the restaurant. Finally, in the restaurant, we were waiting to be seated.

"I want to thank you for being so friendly," said Michelle. "I don't think you noticed, but this is my first time out dressed as a woman. I was shaking with fear in my car when I got to the parking lot. If it wasn't for you being so friendly asking me to get out of the car and holding my hand, I would never have gotten out of my car. I would have driven back home very disappointed."

"Really? I had no inclination," I said. "I am glad my talking put you at ease. Usually most of the time people ask me to shut up."

We followed the hostess to our table. It seemed like all eyes were on us. I heard one male customer say.

"Wow, I haven't seen this many tall women in my life. Where did they all come from?"

This statement made me smile. We were led to a very long table which accommodated us. The wait staff were extremely polite even though they knew some of the women were crossdressers.

At home, Faye wanted to be the wife. It was my responsibility to take on the husband's role which I resented. I was pushed in the corner without a choice. He chose to live as a woman whereas I didn't make the choice to live as a man.

We continued going to the group events. We became good friends with several couples. At times we visited each other outside a group setting. We met for dinner at a restaurant or we stayed home playing cards until 2:00 am. The friendships I developed with these ladies meant a lot to me. They became our extended family. Faye's relationship with the other crossdressers grew stronger.

The group organized a tea party once a year. All the crossdressers and wives wore formal gowns with beautiful hats. It was quite a sight to see. We all glided around the room greeting each other. Several round tables were set up in the room. Each table was covered in white linen that reached the ground. On each table, there was a china teapot.

It was now time for the tea party to begin. We all picked a table to sit. Once we were all seated, a table captain was chosen for each table. The responsibility of the captain was to make sure the teapots were never empty. The captain poured hot tea in china cups for each guest sitting at the table. Delicious crumpets and scones were served made by Destiny (Rodney's wife). She spent hours making the crumpets and scones. They were delicious.

The wives and significant others of the crossdressers' group were very friendly, making it easy to fit in. We sat together toward the back of the room whenever there was a guest speaker that night.

We talked about how our marriages or how our relationships have changed since the cross-dressing. Several of the wives like me had come to terms with this, however, some wives were still bitter. A few of the wives were still having difficulty dealing with their spouse's crossdressing. The changes we experienced in our marriages were very similar. Wives who were bitter and angry found out after being married anywhere from five to thirty years. Even though it was hard on me at the time, I was grateful Jason told me before we were married.

There were still many problems in almost all our marriages. The major problem was often due to the crossdressers' refusal to accept the limitations put on them by their wives. This ultimately resulted in several wives' refusal to support their crossdresser's behavior anymore. The women who initially attempted to understand and cope with their crossdresser lost their sympathetic attitude over time. I was told the longer a woman was in a relationship, the more negative her feelings were towards the crossdresser.

Some of the women said their crossdresser's behavior while crossdressing was gentle, kind, and helpful making it easier to bear. There were others who like me reacted with initial anxiety and then support in the hope that he would "get over it." This hope diminished over time and was replaced by resentment and anger. Every inch we gave to control or limit the crossdressing resulted in a mile taken.

Most of us made the decision to put up with crossdressing provided it did not come to our neighborhood. We didn't want this to hurt our families, friends or our kids. Those were the conditions in order to maintain the marriage. With the increase in the cross-dressing, sex in our marriages and relationships became non-existent. Those wives who disliked or were not interested in sexual activity were not bothered by this aspect of the marriage. For the women like me who still desired sex and were sexually active, the loss of this pleasure left a huge void in our lives.

Deeper and Deeper

I felt very safe going out with Faye for lunch or dinner in the gay neighborhood. We found a little Italian restaurant which we frequented on the weekends. The restaurant hosted a drag show performed by professional drag queens. This was quite interesting and a lot of fun. We became friends with the owner of the restaurant. He treated us special as we were considered regulars. Faye and I would share a meal as we tried to keep our weight and budget down.

One night the restaurant was completely booked so we stood in the hall area waiting for a table. The owner was clearing off a table for us. The owner sat us at a table by the window. The window overlooked a busy street of people walking around the gay neighborhood.

I noticed a nice-looking man standing outside the restaurant looking in at us. Before I knew it, he was in the restaurant walking toward our table. He took the adjacent table. He pulled his chair closer to me and sat down. The man began making light conversation with me.

The man's eyes were fixed on Faye and finally, he spoke to me.

"Tell your friend to smile, she looks too reserved and needs to loosen up."

"Okay, I will pass that on to her," I smiled.

I was trying hard to keep a straight face. I was hoping he would drop the subject about Faye soon. I was unable to warn Faye without him overhearing me. We were all sitting fairly close to each other.

Faye looked over at us and was curious what we were talking about, but didn't give it another thought. The guy spoke again to me.

"Could you ask your friend if she would go out with me for dinner?" Before I could respond he went on, "I'm going to ask her out myself."

He got up from his chair and headed toward Faye's chair. He stood in front of Faye. "You are a beautiful woman. Would you like to go out with me to dinner?"

I couldn't believe what had just happened. My heart was beating so fast I was sure he could hear it. Faye as calm as she could be, pulled me closer to her and responded, "You will need to ask my beautiful wife if it's okay with her."

The guy had no idea Faye was a crossdresser and looked shocked. He turned to me and apologized. "I'm so sorry, I didn't mean to disrespect you. This is my first visit to the gay neighborhood. I had no idea."

"It's okay," I replied. "No worries."

The guy left the restaurant in a hurry. We couldn't believe what just took place. I was always worried any time Faye went out alone. I was afraid if someone like this man at the restaurant approached Faye again, she may not be as lucky as she was today. We were later joined by our friends at the restaurant. We talked about this incident but it was soon forgotten.

I was a part-time beauty consultant. I offered my services free to crossdressers coming out for the first time. They had no idea how to use cosmetic products. I also helped the ones who needed to learn refinement techniques on applying their makeup.

I used my home on weekends to do makeovers. I asked the crossdressers to bring their wigs along with them. I wanted to be sure the wigs suited their faces once the makeup was applied. Invariably I had to recommend a hair salon in Dallas where they could have their wigs trimmed in a style suiting their faces.

I walked them through the application of their makeup so they appeared more feminine. I was always very caring and sensitive to their feelings. I didn't want people laughing or calling out cruel jokes when one of them walked by a crowd of people. I disliked seeing a crossdresser wearing bright-colored eye shadow like teens and young adults wore. They didn't know how to apply the eye shadow well and were often mistaken for drag queens.

This Saturday there were three crossdressers needing makeovers. I welcomed them to my home.

"I will be introducing you to several different products today," I said. "I will teach you how to use these products and techniques while applying them to your face. If you wish to blend in as a woman, remember less is always best."

Straight Talk

We felt it was time to let our sons know about Jason's crossdressing. "Jason, it is important we sit down together when we speak to Joshua and Jude." Jason agreed.

Joshua now twenty-one years old was home from college for the holidays. When he walked in and greeted me he looked around for Jason. "Mom, where's dad?"

"Honey, your dad's at a meeting and should be home soon."

"Why are you not at the meeting?" he asked.

"It's a meeting for men only," I replied.

Joshua burst out laughing. "Mom, Dad is at a crossdressers meeting isn't he?"

I was taken by surprise and started laughing too. "Yes, honey, your dad is at a crossdressers meeting."

Joshua still unable to control his laughter yelled out, "I knew it! I knew it! Dad's a crossdresser, isn't he mom?"

I was always honest with the boys whenever they asked me a question. I nodded. "Yes, your dad is a crossdresser. How did you find out?"

"I saw the crossdressers in our kitchen when I was home on a weekend. You were applying makeup on their faces. I suspected Dad may be one too."

"What are your thoughts on this?"

"I am okay with it, mom. He doesn't drink nor is he physically abusive to you. He's always treated you well. That says a lot about him."

I smiled and hugged my son. I felt blessed that Joshua took the news well. He had no negative feelings towards his dad. I knew he loved his dad very much.

Since Joshua already knew about Jason, I had to tell Jude too. Jude came home shortly after Joshua. Jude who was now nineteen was in the kitchen getting himself a drink. I sat on the stairs leading to his bedroom. I called out to Jude. "Honey, there is something we need to talk about."

Jude looked guilty. "Mom, does this have anything to do with my messy room?"

"No, it doesn't."

"Great." Jude joined me on the stairs.

"Okay, what's up Mom?"

"Jude, your dad's at a men's meeting and should be home fairly soon." I waited for a response from Jude but didn't get one. "All the men at this meeting are heterosexual crossdressers."

"Does this mean our dad is a crossdresser too?"

"Yes, Jude, that's what it means. Joshua found out earlier today about dad being a crossdresser."

Jude laughed. "At the age of seven, I saw large-size women's shoes in dad's closet. I knew they were not yours as you have very small feet. Since then I have always wondered about those large-size shoes. Now I get it." (I remembered telling Jason when the kids were young to put a lock on his closet as I didn't want the kids to see his shoes or girly clothes. He never thought it was necessary since the kids' bedrooms were upstairs.)

"Mom you know dad can't help how he feels," he said. "His brain is wired differently from other men." I should mention Jude was majoring in psychology.

I always taught my sons it was not their place to judge others, and that it was only God who could do this. Nonetheless, I was both surprised and proud to see how well the boys had accepted their dad being a crossdresser.

Later when Jason came home I told him what had transpired with the boys. "The boys know about you being a crossdresser. They have accepted it well."

"It makes me happy they are so accepting of my new life change."

"Jason, the boys love you very much."

At dinner, Jason talked to the boys. "Your mom tells me you know about my crossdressing. Do you have any questions for me?"

Joshua asked. "What do we call you when you are dressed as a female? Do we call you Dad?"

"No, you call me by my female name, Faye."

The boys started to talk about college and the conversation drifted in a different direction.

The Point of No Return

We were members of the crossdresser's group for two years when Faye decided she had outgrown this group. It had become boring for her, she didn't care how I felt. Her desire was to venture out clubbing in the gay neighborhood. There was another group of crossdressers who went out every weekend. They went bar hopping or visited other clubs in the neighborhood.

Faye told me one night at dinner, "Let's join this new group. The ladies are very cool." I knew Faye had already made up her mind and didn't care if I agreed or not.

"You want us to leave the heterosexual crossdressers group to join a group who may not be all heterosexual crossdressers? Faye, I do not like the outfits some of these women wear. Their dresses are so tight and short. If they were to bend down you would see their bottoms."

She used her passive manipulation to change my mind and it always worked. I agreed to this change. I was mad at Faye for not taking my feelings into consideration.

I did everything I could to keep my marriage from falling apart. I constantly remembered my wedding vows made to Jason. This was one of the main reasons I supported Jason's new life as Faye.

I had made friends with the wives in the previous group. They had become very good friends. I was extremely sad to be leaving them. I felt once again I was leaving my friends behind. I would still see them but not on a regular basis. My friends all lived far apart from each other. I felt Faye was being self-centered and selfish again. She took advantage of my being supportive and kept pushing her luck a little too far. She knew I was very faithful to our marriage and felt confident I would never leave her.

I joined Faye several times to events planned on the weekends by this new group. Thelma, one of the crossdressers said, "I wish my wife was supportive to my life as you are to Faye's."

As the crossdressers got to know me better, they enjoyed my company. Some in this new group were rather creepy. Very few of them were still married; most were divorced. Less than a handful were bar hopping with their crossdressers.

Faye went out often to clubs with her new friends. She also started to wear dresses and skirts too short and tight for her. Faye was not concerned with my opinion on what she was wearing anymore. With the stress of seeing Faye dressed and acting up I became sick again. I started to get stressed, my joints flared up and I suffered from frequent migraines. At times I couldn't get off the couch as my body aches were unbearable.

Faye and Jason's personalities were completely the opposite. Faye was flirty, self-centered, selfish, easily irritable and downright rude. She did not care if I was enjoying the night out or not. She wanted to be the center of attention. Faye argued with me every night we went out together. Faye ignored me most of the night and was busy taking photographs; when I looked at the photographs, there was only one of me, way in the background.

Jason was very reserved, calm, caring, and very attentive to me while we were out. He was gentle and very rarely raised his voice at me. Jason hated confrontation and would walk away from an argument rather than deal with it. This behavior caused a lack of communication in our marriage. He loved to hang out with me and the boys watching TV or just being around us. He loved his family. When we were out he was constantly taking pictures of me. He knew I didn't like my pictures taken but did it anyway.

Priorities

Since Jason usually worked on contracts for different companies he was out of work once the contract ended. Sometimes it took several months if not years to find another job. This added financial stress on the marriage and family when he was in between jobs.

Jason was still unemployed and it was a rough three years. This time he became very depressed. He slept most of the day on the couch and was always tired. With so much time on his hands, he became more obsessive about Faye and crossdressing. He got upset when he didn't have money to shop for clothing and accessories for Faye. I felt he should concentrate more on finding a job, buy some decent work clothes for him, and spend less on Faye.

Jason worked in a niche technology support market. The computer hardware and software systems he worked on were a dying industry. He refused to keep up with the current software programs used in companies nationwide. He claimed he didn't like the new computer technology software. He absolutely refused to learn or work on it. This made him non-marketable to companies in the computer industry.

He didn't want to go back to school to update his skills in the computer technology field. It had been years since he used his electrical engineering degree. Therefore, he did not have the current knowledge, skills or experience to be hired as an engineer.

One day Jason talked to me about becoming Cisco CCNA and CCNP Certified. "If I train and receive these certifications, it would make me more marketable and I will command a higher income. To get these certifications, I will need to purchase books that are not cheap. It will cost us around $300.00 or more per book. Do you feel I should do this while looking for a job?"

"Absolutely, go ahead and purchase the books you need."

As an after-thought, I added, "Jason don't you think it would make more sense to enroll in a school to complete these trainings?" In the back of my mind, I knew Jason would slack off if he studied at home. Even though we didn't have the money, I agreed to the purchase of the books.

He purchased the books and began studying. Not even an hour or so into it, he would fall asleep. His naps would last at least an hour. He attempted studying when he was awake only to fall asleep again.

I usually relax in the evenings watching my favorite TV shows. He would join me yet complain to his mother he could not study because I had the TV on. His mother began siding with him against me. Throughout our marriage thus far, she was very objective and didn't take sides. This is what I loved about her.

"Why don't you go to the public library to study if the TV is distracting you?" I said.

"Why should I have to study in a public library when I have a home?"

It was a losing battle with him therefore, I gave up reasoning with him. It was apparent he was just making excuses. He had no intention of completing the courses to get his certifications.

I was right, he didn't complete the courses. The books sat on a shelf collecting dust. He was unable to get a job.

He passively manipulated me to get whatever he wanted. I didn't recognize the signs and mistakenly took it for love. He would cheerfully do almost everything for me. I became extremely dependent on him. This left him in total control of my life. I continued to isolate myself from my family. I was sick most of the time.

The manipulative behavior started whenever I was upset with him for not seriously looking for a job. He always claimed he was on the computer all day sending out resumes. I asked him if he had followed up on any to which his response was negative. He continued to lie to his parents and our friends he was busy job hunting. Our friends were shocked he had not found a job yet since he was so technically savvy.

He left his computer on one day while out for lunch with a friend. I happened to glance at his screen looking for something on his desk. There were a series of text messages between him and his friend. There was a text message in which he confessed he was not looking hard enough for a job. This was the proof I needed to prove he had been lying to me all these years. He enjoyed his fantasy world of dressing as Faye wearing makeup and high-heeled shoes at home. He didn't want to give this up by working in the real world.

We struggled to pay our monthly expenses. We cashed in all our retirement funds which we lived on each month. Jason's parents were very kind and helped us out with our monthly expenses. This was a significant amount of money. I worked on our budget and cut out almost half of our expenses. Jason refused to do a budget or look at what I had put together. Every month when our finances ran low he called his mother asking for help. I asked his mother to stop giving him any more money. She needed to say NO. She made it too easy for him. He lacked the motivation to seriously find a job. He needed to hit rock bottom even though I knew it would drastically hurt our family.

His crossdressing only escalated; that's all he talked about or concentrated on. I was always made to feel guilty for being angry. He was an expert in passive manipulation. This was my second marriage and I did whatever it took to save it from destruction.

Whenever I started a discussion about him finding a job or his crossdressing, he claimed my emotions were out of control. He was going to call my doctor and request an increase in my depression medication. I had a bad track record of discontinuing my medication without consulting my doctor. This didn't make him very happy. Dr. Brown didn't know the real reason I stopped my medications. We could not afford them anymore since we had no health insurance.

Jason went with me to every doctor's appointment. Dr. Brown felt since he was the spouse he would be a better judge of my daily behavior. When he claimed I had extensive mood swings, Dr. Brown increased my dosage which resulted in me becoming overly passive. I quit questioning Jason's decisions even though I didn't agree with them. By this time I was mentally and physically weak. I had no strength left in me to argue with him. Besides what was the point? In his mind, he was always right.

Jason was a procrastinator. He put off doing things that required him to make a decision. He disliked speaking to people on the phone when it came to our bills or anything else. He hated it so much that he would pay the late fees and never question the overcharged amounts on the bills. His mother justified his behavior by saying he got it from her. His dad had to finally take over and make the phone call.

Jason finally applied for a job in a department store. He was offered a part-time job. I was happy he was working. Any income he earned definitely helped our finances.

At the department store, one of his responsibilities was pricing sale items. This included pricing items in the women's department. He enjoyed this very much. He could look at women's clothing and imagine how they would look on him. Now people would not look at him strangely or think he was weird since he worked there.

The first choice of clothing for most crossdressers is experimenting with women's lingerie. One day we were out shopping and of course, he went straight to the lingerie department. He picked out a sexy piece of lingerie and brought it over to show me. I thought it was for me.

"Wow, thank you, honey, it looks great."

"I didn't pick it out for you, it's for Faye."

Realizing what he had just said, as an afterthought he added, "Let's purchase one for you too."

I looked at the price tag and immediately said, "No, we do not have the money for two." He got mad every time I reminded him we didn't have the money to purchase something for Faye.

The department store he worked for hired what he thought was a crossdresser. He went to his boss who was a woman.

"The new employee you hired may be a crossdresser. I can help you relate to this employee as I'm a crossdresser too."

His boss turned red and blushed when he disclosed this information. He came home from work that night extremely happy. "I disclosed to my boss and the other employees I was a crossdresser. They were bound to see me after hours in the lingerie or women's department. I didn't want them to think I was weird."

"I guess the thought never occurred to you to say I am picking something pretty for my wife." I responded sarcastically.

Without my prior knowledge, He disclosed to others that he was a crossdresser. After the fact, he would casually mention it to me as if it didn't matter.

The speakers and psychologists at the group meetings always stressed the importance of speaking to your spouse prior to disclosure at work or other social circles. I was frustrated with him. He didn't care how these disclosures to others would impact my life too.

A Matter of Trust

The only constant in my marriage was my prayers to the lord. I prayed for healing of my mind, body, and soul. I couldn't blame the lord for my circumstances. I acted upon my own free will when I decided to marry Jason. One day I woke up and the cloud in my head began to clear. In its place came clarity of mind and soul. It gave me the will power to change my environment. I decided I was done with being overly medicated and passive. I had left the door open for him to take complete control of my life. It was now time for me to take that control back. I stopped taking the medication without his knowledge.

Finally, I was able to think clearly. I knew there had to be a reason for my illness to progress so rapidly over the years. Running blood or other tests were out of the question since finances and other circumstances didn't allow for this. I was determined to find out why I was sick the past few years.

One morning before I was given my tea in bed I got up and walked to the kitchen. Jason stood over the sink washing my favorite red teapot. On the counter lay a bottle of bleach. He had just poured some bleach into my teapot. He was startled to see me. I confronted him. He said this was the only way to get the teapot and mug clean. I was shocked. I asked how long had this been going on. I didn't get a response. He told me he thoroughly rinsed out the bleach several times in hot water. When there was no trace of bleach left he proceeded to make me my hot tea. At this point, I didn't trust him anymore. I threw away my favorite red tea pot. It was hard to imagine this red tea pot had once given me so much joy and happiness. It ended up being used to bring destruction to my body. I purchased a new tea pot and made my own hot tea in the mornings.

Playing With Fire

We decided to sell our home and move to Dallas. It was hard to imagine we lived in our home for 14 years. There were several reasons for the move. I decided to open an upscale home décor resale store. Our desire was to live closer to the gay neighborhood. We could not afford our house payments any longer.

Jason knew living in the gay neighborhood would remove a significant amount of my stress. He felt I worried too much for his safety when Faye was out alone. We found an apartment in the Bishop Arts District. Jason's parents footed the bill for all our moving expenses to Dallas. I opened my resale store and ran it for two years. He did a significant amount of construction work to get the store ready to open. In the end, I had to close down the store as it wasn't making enough money to support both the apartment and the store.

Our rent was due and we didn't have the money to pay it. Jason asked his mother once again for money to pay the rent. His mother finally said NO.

For the first time in our marriage, Jason was afraid. He had no idea how we were going to pay the rent. I immediately went to my jewelry box and took out all my 22-carat jewelry. I decided to sell the jewelry so we could pay our rent. I made enough money on the sale of my jewelry to pay two months' rent as we were a month behind. It broke my heart to sell my gold necklace with a cross. It was a gift from my godmother for my First Holy Communion. I was seven years old and still remember that day. Every piece of jewelry I sold had a significant emotional value to me. I remember holding the first gold ring I purchased when I was 21 years old. I could feel myself starting to get emotional with tears about to roll down my cheeks. I fought back the tears and emotions even though my heart was breaking. I tried my best not to dwell on these emotions. I told myself I had to do whatever it took to survive. I knew Jason was not capable of helping us financially or in any other way.

Jason worked part-time at the retail store for two years. One day, he was approached by a company whose client was looking for a computer specialist. If he was offered the job he would be earning a fairly decent income again. Once again, I felt a sense of hope. Our financial situation would improve. This job was ideal for him. He would be working from home. Something he had always wanted to do. Jason was offered the job and liked it as he reported to a woman. Jason's boss relied on his technical expertise often. He was thrilled as it made him feel needed. Things were now running fairly well for us.

Then one day he said. "I disclosed to my boss I'm a crossdresser. I am so sorry honey. I should have talked to you first. I sent my boss a link to Faye's site. She wanted to see the pictures."

"I told her I had a beautiful wife." She asked. "Do you have pictures of your wife?" I said. "No my wife doesn't like her pictures taken . . . oh, by the way, honey, I sent her a link to your Facebook page."

This made it the second time he disclosed to a boss that he was a crossdresser prior to my knowledge. The stress and frustration with him continued to grow. I couldn't believe he had sent his boss a link to my Facebook page. He had become a crossdressing time bomb waiting to explode.

The income he was earning was more than what he had been making in quite a while. Yet the fear of losing his job didn't seem to concern him. I knew he was playing with fire. Eventually, our family would get burnt if he continued with this type of behavior. When I communicated my fears to him, he just brushed it off as no big deal.

Birthdays were very important to me. Our birthdays were usually celebrated as a family. This included Grandma and Grandpa who were his parents. This year, Faye (Jason) decided to celebrate her birthday at a club with some of her new cross-dresser friends. I was extremely hurt. Faye had set this up before letting me know. I decided not to go. This didn't seem to bother her.

I was sad not to be with her on her birthday. I asked Joshua and Jude, "Do you want to go to the club where Dad is celebrating his birthday?" They agreed fairly quickly. The three of us drove to the club in Joshua's car. When we arrived she was surprised to see us, however, there was no excitement on her face. She introduced us to her friends. She chatted with us for a few minutes and then disappeared.

We spent an hour or more talking to her friends. We were tired and ready to go home. We looked for Faye but didn't see her. Her friend suggested we look on the dance floor. When we got to the dance floor, she was alone. She was standing by the dance floor waiting for an invitation to dance.

"We are tired and ready to go home," I said.

All she said was, "Good-bye."

I was very disappointed and hurt. We had taken the time to be there for her. She treated us like we were perfect strangers. I knew Jason would never do something like this. The three of us left the club without saying a word. By this time Faye was living her life as though she was single.

The Games People Play

Faye was staying up late every night. She was sending messages to people on Facebook. She was also visiting strange websites. Whenever I walked in the room Faye minimized the computer screen.

"Why did you minimize your screen when I walked in?"

She denied this. "You're crazy I didn't do that."

"Faye I'm not your mother. You have no reason to lie to me. I am not concerned which websites you visit, nor who you chat with. I'm more concerned this activity keeps you up till 3:00 am in the morning. You are a grouch the next day and difficult to live with. You are not getting enough sleep. You complain to your mother that I'm the cause of this. It is time for you to grow up and cut the apron strings."

I could not handle Faye lying to me. As far as I knew she had never done this before. She was laying the foundation for a deadly game and I was her target. This proved to be true when I read one of her text messages which I printed between her and her friend.

Faye sent a text to her friend saying, "I think she's (me) on the phone with her oldest brother. Once she falls asleep, I will look at her call log to be sure that's who it was. I need to call him and convince him she needs to be committed."

I confronted Faye. "I printed out the text messages between you and your friend. You are playing a sick game. Good luck convincing my family to have me committed. It is not going to happen so don't even try it."

Through all the ups and downs of my marriage, I stayed faithful to Faye (Jason). I kept reminding myself of my wedding vows. I seriously felt my responsibility was to stand by my man no matter how bad things were. The mental abuse is so much more destructive than the verbal and physical abuse.

Almost all of the heterosexual crossdressers I met were very protective of their wives or significant others' privacy. They usually left home at night wearing a disguise over their female clothing. They selected a suitable disguise to avoid exposing their identity to maintain their wives' or significant other's identity. They very rarely left home during the day.

Faye did not wear a disguise when she went out nor did she restrict herself to going out only at night. I understood and was sensitive towards Faye's desire to be accepted as a woman. However, I resented her for compromising mine and our sons' privacy by bringing herself into our neighborhood. Several people in the neighborhood who saw her knew it was Jason. They made fun of her behind her back.

Faye invited me to go bar hopping with her friends on the weekends. I refused the invitations as I was upset with her for coming out openly in our neighborhood. Faye went out every weekend with her friends. She put off going to visit her parents. Her crossdresser's events were more important. If she visited her parents she would have to go in guy mode dressed as Jason. Her parents were unaware of their son being a crossdresser.

I noticed for a couple of weeks Faye seemed happier than she had been in a long time. She kept talking about a new crossdresser friend she had just met named Felicia. Faye said. "You are probably tired of always hearing me talk about my new friend. "

"That's fine with me," I replied. "I am happy to hear you communicate your feelings for your friend to me. You have always had a hard time expressing your feelings as you kept them to yourself. It has been a long time since we have communicated on such a deep level."

Faye went on to say, "Felicia has helped me overcome my insecurities and tells me how feminine and pretty I look."

I stopped her right there saying, "I have been doing and saying the same things to you all these years. I have supported you as a crossdresser for fifteen years.

"Faye, you speak of this person as you used to of me when we first met. Are you in love with this person?"

"Maybe or maybe not," she said, with a smile on her face. "I'm definitely attracted to Felicia and have feelings for her. Please be patient with me while I get this all sorted out in my mind. Felicia does not feel the same way about me. This relationship is not going anywhere since Felicia is also married too. She has no intention of leaving her wife."

After a bit, Faye shocked me with, "All Felicia and I did was exchange a kiss and that's all."

"Do you realize what you are saying, Faye?" *I was horrified.*

She tried to squirm her way out of this like a snake, but she knew she had said way too much already.

"Do you realize you kissed a man?" I asked.

"No, I kissed a woman named Felicia and not a man," Faye kept repeating this over and over again. Finally, she stopped. "I felt very uncomfortable when I kissed her. It felt like I was cheating on you."

"Yes, Faye, you were cheating on me. The fact you had feelings for another person was enough to tell you this was not right. All you had to do was tell me and we could have arranged to get a divorce. I definitely do not want to be with a person who isn't in love with me anymore. However, instead, you chose to be a coward by drugging me, wishing to convince my brother I needed to be committed, making me physically ill by using bleach to clean my teapot and tea cups, and telling your parents how you were being mistreated by me.

"You never came to my defense when your mother was blaming me all these years for the problems we were having in our marriage. In fact, you agreed with her. I could have yelled back at your mother and told her exactly what was going on in our marriage. I just didn't have the heart to hurt her. Even though she tore me apart, out of respect for her I couldn't tell her you were a crossdresser. You were so afraid of your mother, you didn't have the guts to ask me for a divorce."

When I thought things couldn't get any worse than what they were, Faye blamed me for the affair with Felicia.

"If you had only gone out with me on the weekends, this would never have happened. I was so lonely without you. I fell into the arms of another woman for comfort."

Faye continued to blame me. "You should have set boundaries for me when I went out alone."

"You are not a child," I said. "I shouldn't have had to set boundaries for you. You are a grown adult who knows right from wrong. You did it anyway, so don't blame me for your infidelity. You blame me for everything that goes wrong. You refuse to accept responsibility for your own actions."

Faye tried hard to convince me.

"I still love you and will come home to you every night. I am not going anywhere else. I am not gay and still want to be with you."

I was emotionally drained by this discussion. It took me weeks to get over Faye's infidelity. I loved Jason very much and did not want my marriage to end.

"I am going to meet Felicia for lunch," Faye told me. "Both of us will be dressed in guy mode. I want to find out if this attraction is even real."

When Jason came home from lunch he seemed relieved.

"Everything is okay. I am not attracted to Felicia as a man at all."

"What does this mean? Are you no longer attracted to Felicia his feminine side?"

"My feelings for Felicia have not changed. I am still trying to sort these feelings out in my mind."

This caused more confusion for me since Jason was not a full-time crossdresser at this point. I agreed I would give him more time to work through these feelings.

Faye told me she was going to a club which Felicia and a group of other crossdressers thought she might like. This was a club where people lived out their fantasies. At this club, they inflicted pain on each other for sexual pleasure with a willing partner. Felicia was no stranger to this club. Felicia told Faye to call her anytime she wanted to live out her fantasy she would be Faye's willing partner.

I already knew Jason liked the fetishistic life. I was opposed to this type of sexual play. I had communicated this to Jason when he brought it up when we first met. Jason was very considerate of my feelings and did not push the issue with me.

Faye now began being very honest with me. She told me about Felicia volunteering to be her sexual play partner. At first, I was not opposed to this. Faye suggested I keep an open mind and go with her to check this new place out. When Faye told me what a sexual partner did, I quickly changed my mind.

"Faye, if anyone's going to inflict pain on you for your sexual pleasure it will be me, not Felicia."

We arrived at the place. I immediately started to tense up and get nervous; Faye told me she was nervous too as this was her first time to a place like this. We were welcomed in and led to a large room. This room was where all the play took place. There were different types of play equipment laid out neatly. For those who wanted to participate in play, the ground rules were explained.

Once they were done explaining the rules. The fear set in and I began to get afraid when I saw all the play equipment. There were several people already in the room engaged in play. It was hard for me to believe this pain could be enjoyable. There were two huge wooden crosses mounted flush against one wall. On the other side of the room, there were makeshift wooden beds. The beds consisted of planks of wood placed horizontally across, supported, and attached to wooden vertical support legs.

On one of the beds, there was a woman tied up face down and her partner was spanking her with what looked like a flat lightweight paddle. There were also other objects used which I did not stick around to see. There was another woman who was screaming extremely loud. It seemed like all the visitors moved towards the screams. We found a woman tied up off the floor in what looked like a cage made of ropes with large loops. Her partner was under the rope cage beating her bottom with what appeared to be a bat. The woman's bottom was filled with blisters which had turned blue. We were told she was screaming out of pleasure. She was enjoying this type of play. I told Faye I needed to move away as I couldn't bear to watch this anymore.

The woman on the bed who was been spanked eventually reached a state of sub-consciousness. Her partner carried her off the bed and cradled her on a couch to bring her gently back to consciousness. In this play, the partner could have been a spouse, significant other, friend, or a person she hired to spank her.

I was told by another person in the room it was common for the play partners to share an intimate sexual relationship outside their marriages. The partners' relationship continued often without the wife or significant other's knowledge.

I quickly realized this place was frequented by many of the married crossdressers. Most of their wives or significant others had no idea their crossdressers were engaged in this type of sexual pleasure. The ones that knew had no interest in going along. They preferred their crossdresser to just go and do their own thing.

I knew that Faye was not capable of separating her feelings easily. She could very easily end up emotionally and physically involved with her partner. Faye indicated she would prefer to have me as her partner. She felt this may enhance our marriage. She was truthful and honest with me when it came to her fantasy. She wanted me to inflict pain on her as it gave her a sexual release and satisfaction.

We were there for several hours and I had enough. I told Faye this was not what I wanted in my marriage so we decided to leave.

Faye dropped me off to a local bar where her crossdresser friends were gathering. She could not stay as she had a class to attend. The plan was to join me once she was done with the class. That night I met Teresa, a crossdresser friend of ours. Teresa was in the process of transitioning to becoming a woman. She had been financially planning to have the surgery done for quite some time. She looked really sad and upset. "What's wrong, Teresa, you look so sad. Why are you crying?"

"My lover is a heterosexual crossdresser just like me. He is married to a genetic woman. He broke up our relationship to save his marriage. I feel so betrayed." I knew exactly the person and his wife she was talking about.

Teresa took me totally by surprise when she asked, "Does Faye show any signs of gay tendencies?"

I immediately said, "No."

I hesitated for a few minutes. "Teresa, why did you ask me that question?"

"It is typical for most crossdressers to become involved in gay relationships."

"Faye told me she has feelings for Felicia and she may or may not be in love with her. She said it was just a kiss, but I don't believe her. I think they shared more than a kiss."

Now I was crying. "Teresa, I do not understand Faye and Felicia's relationship."

"Honey, that girl has nothing over you. She is a tramp and a bimbo. Everybody in the gay community knows this."

One night Faye invited me to have dinner with Felicia and another couple to prove there wasn't anything between them. As we were getting out of the car, Faye pointed me in the direction of a woman wearing a blue suit.

"That's Felicia walking down the street towards the restaurant."

Faye looked very happy and excited. It was hard not to miss. When we were seated in the restaurant. I got a better glimpse of Felicia's outfit. It was made of some sort of weird plastic fabric. The skirt flared out and under the skirt, she had a stiff netting fabric holding it up. The skirt was way too short. She wore long lacey underwear which was very visible. It left nothing to the imagination. She knew her underwear was showing but didn't care. She loved the attention she was getting in the restaurant even though it was negative.

I do not know who Faye is anymore. There was definitely no Jason left.

Weeks went by and Faye continued to chat with her friends. She continued to minimize the computer screen when I walked in the room.

There were times Faye left the house when she received a phone call. I would later see her in the car talking to somebody with the car doors locked. Seeing her being so secretive only increased my anxiety level.

I started to get paranoid with Faye's behavior and was upset with her most of the time. I didn't trust Faye anymore. I knew she was lying to me often. This behavior of Faye's continued. I was suffering with pain from a broken heart. I didn't want her to know how much she truly hurt me with her affair with Felicia.

The End

Things changed in the last six months of our marriage. This was when Felicia showed up in our lives (though I knew in my heart the attraction to Felicia would fade away in time.)

I was the first girl Faye seriously dated. I knew she did not experience the parties and fun I did as a teenager. Faye was living the life Jason had missed as a teenager. For the first time in her life, she was having fun. She bragged about making new friends on her own without my help. She looked forward to the weekends so she could party with her friends.

Faye came up with an agreement. This would allow Faye to be carefree with limitations. She could spend time with other crossdressers provided things were handled appropriately.

I felt Faye was the other woman in Jason's life. He was very obsessed with his feminine side. I felt Jason's feelings for Faye were stronger than they were for me. His interest was in what Faye wanted to do rather than what I wanted to do.

While Faye was out one weekend with her friends, I stayed home and watched my favorite TV shows. This particular night I was up till Faye got home which was 2:00 am. She saw me sitting on the couch.

"You are so boring and have no friends," was all she had to say.

I looked at her in disgust.

"Faye I do not need to go bar hopping every weekend in my fifties. I am very comfortable with who I am. You seem to be gender-confused. You are spending money every weekend, money that we don't have. My outgoing and bubbly personality was crushed years ago. No person should have to experience these difficulties in their marriage."

The life I knew changed so drastically and was propelling downwards at such a high speed. This made it difficult for me to come to terms with Faye's indiscretions. Her refusal to see a psychologist with me made it impossible to address any problems in our relationship. She was agreeable to go only if it helped me admit I was the cause of all the problems in our marriage, not her. Faye did not believe in a separation period.

"If you want to leave you might as well file for divorce."

I knew my marriage was over and there was no sense in prolonging the misery. I told Jason I wanted a divorce and at first he didn't agree, he felt we could work this out. Jason knew I did not trust him anymore. I felt very strongly if you couldn't trust your spouse the marriage was over.

We completed the divorce paperwork together and I filed for divorce without an attorney. I looked forward to a peaceful life without dealing with Jason or Faye anymore.

It was all over. The divorce was granted and my marriage of fifteen years was gone in a flash. What a sense of freedom for me. I didn't think I would ever feel this free again. I called Jason up and told him I had just returned from the courthouse. I said. "It's official we are no longer husband and wife."

I look back at my fifteen-year marriage to Jason and knew I did everything I could to save my marriage. I was walking away with bittersweet memories.

Since I celebrated my marriage fifteen years ago with friends and a party, it was only fitting to celebrate my divorce.

I threw a party celebrating my newfound freedom. I picked the Bar of Bishop to have my party. I invited my friends to join in the celebration. Most of my friends had never heard of a divorce party.

I was so excited on the day of the party. I was going to wear the dress I bought especially for this night. It was a slim, clingy dress that showed off my curves. My friends joined me at the bar and celebrated the end of my marriage. Joshua and Jude were at the party too which made me very happy. They too joined in the celebration. They were excited to see me happy and having a good time.

The DJ played the song "I Am a Survivor," especially for me several times that night. I danced solo to this song and acted it out. The DJ and my friends were laughing with me.

I felt confident that God was with me. Once again, he snatched me out of a marriage that was no longer good for me.

I have survived the three years since my divorce from Jason/Faye. I have embraced the new 'normal.' I am no longer taking several of the medications I was put on. My illnesses disappeared soon after the divorce.

These days I stay home and volunteer when needed. Joshua bought a home. Jude and I live with him. We love the relationship we have with each other. I cherish the independence, living as a single woman, and most especially the absence of all the "high drama" that came with living with Faye.

Faye is now in a relationship with another transgender who lives as a man and dresses as a female. To this day Faye will not admit she is gay, even though she is in a sexual relationship with a man. I was prescribed estrogen pills after my hysterectomy. The doctor advised me to stop taking them as they made me extremely emotional. Unknown to me, Faye was taking the leftover pills. She was bragging about developing breasts. She then told me what she had done. By this time I shook my head and moved on. I do not have an update on whether Faye is going through any other transitions to become a woman or not. She has legally changed her gender marker to "female" and has changed her driver's license too. We have not spoken to each other in over a year and I have no desire to change that.

AFTERWORD

There are many women who are forced to keep their relationships with their heterosexual crossdressers or significant others a secret. Not because their husbands or significant others are crossdressers, but because our society has issues accepting and understanding crossdressing.

There are many heterosexual crossdressers living in our country that have chosen to come out of the closet. They have suffered discrimination at the hands of an unaccepting society.

Most heterosexual crossdressers love and cherish their marriages and relationships with women and children. In most cases, these men do not want to become women. They are secure in their masculine and feminine sides. These were the heterosexual crossdressers in our first group.

My prayer is that the day will come when society accepts crossdressers as decent loving human beings. My hope for the future is marriages to heterosexual crossdressers are embraced by their families, friends, and society.

Unfortunately, crossdressers are discriminated against by their own families. Their families are ashamed of their crossdressers and choose to cut ties with them completely. Families are more concerned about what their church friends and neighbors will think rather than learn more about cross-dressing. Gaining this knowledge will help them understand their crossdresser a lot better. Crossdressers need the love and support of their families.

I already had a strong relationship with Christ. I sought his guidance through prayer and meditation in this difficult marriage. I firmly believe the Holy Spirit speaks to us in the form of a little voice buried deep down in our core being. He provides us with the answers to our prayers. All we need to do is be still and listen quietly to that voice.

About the Author

Noreen Antao enjoyed a successful sales career in Corporate America, where she honed her communications skills. Her empathy for people suffering injustices, particularly those whose life is considered taboo by society, moved her to use those skills to write this book. She is also the biographer who ghostwrote "The Life and Legend of Robert 'Stonewall' Jackson."

Noreen is a Christian Indian whose family came from the State of Goa, India's smallest state, which is situated on the Arabian Sea. She was born in Karachi, Pakistan, and immigrated to the USA in 1981, where she immediately went to work in sales. She and her family reside in Texas.